To Kate,

Always be guided

By the light

Within your heart

Love

Mitch xx

M.G.C

Spirit Magick

A Practical Guide To Psychic and Mediumship Development

By

Mitch Garlington

Sometimes The Hardest Part Of The Journey Is Believing You're Worthy Of The Trip - Jade Kyle

Contents

Introduction	1
The Gift	3
The Spirit Realm	8
Lightworker	15
Your Spiritual Journal	20
Trust	22
Ego	29
Breaking Free from the Matrix System	38
Sitting Within the Power	45
Energy	49
The Chakra System and the Seven Major Chakras	57
The Psychic Body	63
Your Spirit Team	75
The Power of the Spiritual Medium	88
Understanding the Clairs	93
Grounding, Earthing, Opening and Closing Ritual	102
Structure of a Message from Spirit	116
Creating a Spirit Key	121
Psychic vs. Mediumship	129
Evidence	135
Protection	141
Ethics of Spiritualism – Code of Conduct	160
Staying Authentic	166
Unconditional Love	174
Blessings	178

Introduction

Dear Reader,

Thank you and welcome for being guided to purchase this book. When I first started my own spiritual journey, I found it very hard to make sense of my gifts. The information wasn't as freely available as it is becoming in this new world. My learnings and teachings were gathered from various places, such as open development circles, spiritual gatherings, teachings from various mentors that came into my life, and my own research and intuition. It often felt like I was gifted a big jigsaw puzzle and slowly but surely, I was piecing together all the parts to make up one clear picture.

I found it very frustrating at times (it often felt like important pieces of this jigsaw puzzle were missing) and I would question myself; was I working correctly? or in danger of doing things wrong? was I good enough and really connecting to the higher realms of light or just talking a lot of old rubbish?

As time went on I realised that everything works on the vibration of unconditional love and correct intention - as long as you have these two key pieces in place, you cannot and will not go wrong.

This book is a practical guide to understanding psychic and mediumship development, through the eyes of a full time Spiritual Medium - Psychic -

Tarot Reader... Mitch Garlington. I wanted to create a book of truth that covered everything to help make sense and make it easier for other people, when they are tapping into and developing their personal and own gift.

Development is a personal journey of discovery; do not compare yourself to another, for you hold within your heart, your own unique magick. Timescales vary from person to person, for some development happens quickly, whilst with others it can take months or even years. The key thing to remember is always be gentle on yourself.

Development is a lifelong process - like an artist that is never quite satisfied with their latest painting...

I can only talk about the ways, teachings and techniques I have found work best for me. I hope you will enjoy the learnings I have covered. Use the information within this book wisely to act as a platform or foundation for developing your own gifts and tapping into your own magick.

Blessed Be Dear Reader

Mitch x

The Gift

You will often hear the term 'he or she has the gift' or 'is gifted' but what does this actually mean?

The truth is we are all gifted and have the gift on some level. When a person is said to be 'gifted' or spiritually awoken it means that they have started to invest the time back into themselves. This can range and vary in many ways - it could be a person feels trapped within a relationship, a work situation, or some other area of their world, and they are taking the needed steps to remove the unwanted energy and make lifelong changes. This may also be through various forms of self-development, or a personal healing journey, say for instance someone may have fought a battle with cancer or other illness, survived an accident, had an out of body experience, conquered some form of abuse or addiction or some other form of healing journey, that has stirred and awoken them from their slumber. They basically start to see the world with new eyes...

It is often said that children are the most spiritually gifted, awoken souls that walk the earth. They are pure souls that have not yet been conditioned into the structure and manipulation of the physical world.

I am a firm believer we are all born equal and no one is above another. We all breathe the same way; we all bleed the same way. We are all one and connected to the universal energy or web of life. Yet we all have the power of freewill and this greatly determines how a person chooses to be within this lifetime.

When we enter into this world, we are pure souls that have been sent from the spirit realm. But as time goes on, we start to become conditioned and the demands of the physical world are put upon us. Depending on our own upbringing, this can greatly amplify or hinder a person's gift. As time goes on some of us will basically lose touch with our higher self, as we become conditioned, this means we forget all the learnings and teachings we would have come to know and learnt from being in the spirit realm and previous lifetimes before. Often, we forget the basics and have no understanding or knowledge of how to work within our own psychic or spiritual body, so we have to start again within this lifetime and retrain ourselves to understand. (This is often what is known as breaking free from the matrix system - we will learn more on this later).

Spiritually awoken souls have usually (although not always) had a rough ride. Often, they have had to deal with a lot more pain and suffering in one shape or form then the average person. They will often feel like the outcast, the outsider that doesn't seem to fit in anywhere, the freak or weird person no one wants to be associated with. They can be the old soul on young shoulders, the loner, the empath, the black sheep that can feel the pain of everyone and everything around them.

To be gifted is not for the faint hearted. Often, it's a gift you have not asked for but it's in your DNA and its part of who you are. It can, at times, if not be controlled correctly, feel like a curse.

The truth, however, is all about vibration...

We all vibrate on a level of frequency... everything holds energy and has a vibration of its own. From the chair you are sitting in, to this book you are holding. For those of you that like science, this is a scientifically proven fact and there have been many books written in depth on this subject matter alone.

When a person is gifted... they vibrate on a higher level or frequency and their place of self-awareness is much more amplified than that of someone that has not yet awoken to their true spiritual potential.

This is usually why gifted souls struggle with the everyday world. Often, they are around people on a much lower vibration or frequency level... in return the gifted soul has to lower their vibration down to 'fit into' the world around them. This is not good and can ultimately come at a cost to the gifted soul's overall state of wellbeing. It's almost like forcing your feet to fit into a pair of size eight shoes, when you're really a size ten. Your feet may cope in the short term, but long term they would hurt and in time do long lasting damage.

You may be asking yourself right now 'Why do those with the gift have to lower their vibration?'

When we change our level of energy or vibration, we also learn something new. Each vibration carries a lifelong learning or lesson with it therefore, someone on a lower frequency would never be able to match that of a gifted soul. Quite simply they have not yet learnt the particular lesson they need to in order to amplify on that particular level of frequency or state of awareness. However, the gifted soul has already learnt the lessons of the lower levels, so it is easier for them to change their vibration downwards. This is something you will naturally do every day, and you may not always be aware you are doing it. But as your personal development journey grows, you will become more aware within yourself. When you need to do this, you will also be able to put a protection in place that won't affect your own state of wellbeing.

You may already be starting to think about this... and see this pattern within your own world?

This is often why we encounter problems with people around us. When we are 'gifted' it can feel like a moth to a flame. Almost like everyone around you can see your inner light or frequency before you do. This will naturally divide opinion; some people will feel comfortable with your frequency but pay attention to those that may try to abuse the situation. Some people will not be able to handle your light and that is OK, but it may cause hostility towards you for no apparent reason. This is what is known as the mirrored effect. You may have worked through something that they are currently unable to do and so you are mirroring to them the lesson they need to learn, to raise their own vibration. When this happens, you may become subjected to emotional garbage, or drama. Just send the energy in question love, as love is what they are lacking in their own frequency level to overcome the obstacle that is blocking them.

Also be aware of others that try to absorb you or want you to walk for them. People can sometimes use your energy level like a battery charger for their own personal gain. (This is known as energy vampires and psychic attack; we will learn more about this later). Sometimes people are not even aware they are behaving in this way.

Have you ever felt drained from someone around you, but never really understood why? They may seem on the face of things a lovely person, yet when you're in their presence for too long they leave you feeling tired and burnt out or low of all energy?

When I did my own development, this was touched on but never fully explained to me. It was something I was becoming aware of and had to puzzle together for the most part myself. Then, I later asked mentors and they confirmed the above. This is why I have put this as a starting point to the book as it makes so much sense to me on a personal level, and I feel it is really a key ingredient for anyone wanting to develop their own gift and power.

Growing up as a child I always felt on the edge of a circle looking in. If I had known back then, 'Mitch, it's OK you just vibrate on a higher frequency than the muggles around you', things may have been different. But I am also a firm believer in everything happens for a reason in the right space and time. That period of my life was not the correct time to fully embrace my gift or the spirit world, even though the power of spirit was already working with me behind the scenes…

People Fall Out Of Your Life As Your Frequency Rises... Let Them Go. This Is Part Of Your Frequency Rising - Galactic Yadira

The Spirit Realm

As a spiritual medium people often ask me "What is spirit?" or "What happens in the spirit world or spirit realm?"

Again, as I have already said I can only talk about this subject from my own level of awareness and understanding. Like you, I am also developing my gifts. Development is a bit like peeling back an onion, every time you feel you have got it, you are suddenly shown another layer you hadn't noticed before. Revealing or linking something deeper than that of the last layer, a new lesson to be gifted and learnt. You may find the following sits correctly with you or you may disagree with some of it and that is OK. I can only talk about the firsthand accounts I have been blessed to witness through my own spirit work and from my own spirit team.

Who are we?

We are a spiritual being descended from the higher realms of light and universal energy, a star. We have been sent back to Earth and given the gift of physical form, to develop, to learn and grow, to pay back any karma debts we may carry from previous lifetimes before and to love and live the gift of life...

We are spirit and our body is a vessel, a car, the mode of transport that gets us from A to B whilst we are here in this physical 3D lifetime.

As I have already mentioned we all work on a frequency vibration. Depending on how we act determines what vibration we give out into the world. If you are someone that is very negative and has a low outlook on the world around them, you are going to be working on a low vibration. This is what is known as negative energy. Whereas if you are someone that is very happy, upbeat, has a healthy outlook to the world around them, you will be on a much higher frequency positive energy. This in effect is what is known as the yin and yang energy that makes up the world we live in. What we send out we get back. Like attracts like. This state of being also determines what happens when our physical body dies. How we live in this lifetime carves the footprints for the next life, be mindful of your actions.

What happens when we die?

When our vessel or body starts to let us down, it is preparing the spirit within for a new journey – a journey back home to the spirit world. As our physical body dies, the spirit, the soul essence within, lives on... and a bit like a door being opened, the spirit can no longer use the existing vessel so is set free. Free to journey home once more to the spirit realm.

When I have given messages both in a demonstration setting and on a one to one level. A common theme spirit talk to the receiver of the message about is 'there was no pain'. It is my belief from what I have been made aware of time and time again that, the spirit will always try to leave the body, prior to the physical body shutting down. In circumstances of a car crash, suicide or other tragedy again from what I have been made aware of, spirit will leave the vessel before the vessel takes impact. With this theory in mind what we must remember is, whilst the physical body may have suffered, the spirit, the soul essence, the energy of a person's soul that is eternal has already left and is venturing home. So, there isn't any pain to the soul/spirit energy. You will hear of nurses, and staff within care homes, and other professions saying they can sense a person has gone, before they are actually pronounced dead. This is my understanding as to why.

It has also been known within mediumship for people that suffer with severe dementia, to have the ability to almost dip in and out of the two worlds. I know of several mediums, and myself that have given readings where the spirit has come through with clear evidence. But they have not actually yet passed. Once more proving that the spirit or soul is whole and intact, and it is sadly the results of their body or vessel not working correctly or shutting down.

What happens when the spirit goes?

When the spirit is set free it will travel home to the spirit realm. I believe that the spirit realm is made up of layers or levels of light. I do not believe in a 'heaven and hell' but I do believe in a realm where other realms coexist. Light and dark. We must remember that as with this lifetime there is light and dark, good and bad. So, it stands to reason this will continue in the next realm. It is my understanding that spirits that may have lived a life in darkness and evil, will be for a time in what is known as a healing realm. This will be a place of solitude to reflect and make sense of what may have happened and why they carried out the actions they did. There are occasions where spirits may not want to transition to the light, and so they choose to stay here. This is often what becomes known as trapped spirits, and often will result in poltergeist or negative energy or activity.

The spirit is scared to move on for fear of judgement and what might await them in the next life. So, they choose to stay stuck in a world they do not belong in and haunt the shadows of the past. This is often why a place or object becomes 'haunted' and can seem scary. For those that like to go on ghost hunts, this is the type of spirit you may encounter. You are putting yourself in the position to make contact with an angry or frustrated spirit that does not want to take account or responsibility for the actions they made whilst they were alive.

For the most part however, the spirit will transition to the light, and will reconnect with loved ones, family members, animals and friends. This will be a place of pure unconditional love and peace.

What we must remember at this stage is spirit do not have physical form, they leave that behind when the body dies. It is that light from within that the spirit is and becomes. The spirit realm is a higher level of frequency.

When you see pure sunlight shining in through a window and it makes you feel whole and happy that's how I perceive spirit to be. Spirit is made up of pure light energy and is always around us. Remember they do not have physical form anymore. This is why if you are lucky enough to see a spirit they often, although not always, look like a smoky mist, they are showing themselves how they looked when in physical form through an image and shadow of light. Or you may witness small orbs, again this is spirit letting you know they are around.

For spirits that may have been involved in some type of tragedy, they will enter a healing realm to regain strength and purity, before fully embracing the spirit world, and again they will connect with loved ones in the realm of unconditional love, light and eternal peace.

Time

This is something I am asked so often as a medium. "How long before a person can come through and make contact?" It's really like asking someone "how long is a piece of string?" The truth is time is manmade. It's something we have created to keep a structure in place within the physical world. The real truth is that time does not really exist, look how easily we manipulate time when we move a clock backwards or forwards. Time does not exist in the spirit world. What is more important is to look at the behaviours of the spirit themselves...

What I mean by this is what was the person's faith in life? their personality? were they spiritual and in tune with the world around them? or were they a person that was very logical and didn't believe in anything else past physical death? These factors will play a part when and if a spirit person can make contact. This is something that sadly is completely outside of a medium's control. We can never click and link a person in, it is all on spirit's terms. Any medium that says otherwise in my opinion is not working from true spirit source, but from their own ego.

I firmly believe that if a spirit person is able to make contact, they will always find a way to let a receiver know they are safe. They do not always make contact with the person direct, sometimes they will message grab through a friend or other family member. But where possible they will try to give reassurance they are safe and at peace.

(For those of you that may have read my second book "Stranger In This World", you will see I talk about an experience in which spirit used me as an in-between person. To get a message to my partner that his Mum was home safe in the spirit world).

I have been blessed to provide readings, where unknown to me a person has passed days before and been able to give accounts on what they want their funeral to be like, songs to be played, where they want the ashes laid to rest etc.. I have also had the opposite, where a client has come for a reading, and the loved one may have been gone for months or even years. But for reasons we will never know they just have not been able to make contact. Often in these situations every other family member, friend, and animal will step forward to give the sitter validation that their loved ones are safe. But that one person they are seeking is just not able to link in at that time.

Therefore, I always say to people don't get caught up in time and don't focus on wanting one particular person to come forward. It's really irrelevant and time is something that gets left behind in the physical world when spirit transition.

What do spirits do when they move on?

This is something that often people ponder about. Again, it really goes back to frequency. Depending how a person has lived in this lifetime will determine what happens to them when in the spirit realm. If a person has lived a life with a good heart and tried their best to send love to the world, they will have the option to stay in the spirit world. Now remember as I have already stated there is no time in the spirit world. So, they may stay there, and it may feel like weeks or months but in reality, could be years.

They will often stay and reconnect with loved ones that have gone before and go after. In time they may have the option to become a spirit guide or door keeper or be reincarnated if they choose or want to live a new life. Or they may choose to just stay in the realm of spirit, the vibration of unconditional love and light.

However,

For those souls that have transitioned on a lower level, they will not have the same choices. If a person has done bad or evil things when they transition, they will incur a karma debt. It is my belief from what spirit have shown me that this is unavoidable, and they must learn from the error of their wrong doings. They will at some point be reincarnated and sent back to Earth to relive a life. This will not be optional; they will have no say in the matter; however it will not be instantly. Once reincarnated they will have the power to correct and learn from the mistakes that were made before. It might be that they choose to make the same mistakes again and so the cycle will continue, until the life lessons are learnt. Once this happens frequency levels change bringing in new options.

There are various religions that each believe in a slightly different format or cycle of life. For those that have read my other books you will know that I am a solitary male witch. I do not believe in a set religion as such. I believe, like in the tarot, death is not the end it's just the closing of one chapter and the start of something new. Death is often a rebirth. Like the tree of life, we are all connected and whilst the cycle continues the frequency changes. Allowing us to become time travellers almost exploring different realms, and universes within our own state of consciousness. We are the door keepers of our own destiny. Death is merely a doorway to new beginnings and a new world.

In The Spiritual Realm, The Opposite Of Ignorance Is Not Knowledge, It's Obedience - Howard G Hendricks

Lightworker

Before we move forward and look at development itself, I feel it's important to talk about the work of a lightworker. When I first started out like a lot of 'gifted' souls the gift really found me. It can be a scary, confusing place to be in at times. Often people don't really talk about the lead up to development and at times you can feel like you are actually going crazy.

Before I properly took the steps to make sense of my gifts, I often would see spirits within my previous working world with customers. Or I would pick up on the emotions or energies of people around me, at times these feelings felt overwhelming. It could sometimes feel like I was inside a person's head hearing all these different thought patterns. Sometimes my hands would be boiling hot if a person had an illness, or hurt themselves, I later realised this was healing energy, and had I known how to channel that I could have offered that person healing.

What we must remember is spirit has chosen to work with us. It's very scary to put trust into something we cannot always physically see. So often whilst part of us is aware, we may choose to go the long way around in our development journey.

I was told many years ago I would be a successful working medium, yet it took me six years later from being told that to actually doing something about it and train and develop my own gift!

You yourself may have been aware you have a gift on some level, but you may also be scared or wary to tap into the full extent or power that you possess. Do not fear this, instead embrace and nurture the lightworker within you. By doing this you will open up worlds you didn't even know you had access too.

Lightworker?

The term lightworker is someone that works from a pure heart for the highest of good in all they do. Often, they will go without for others around them, even if it ends up being at a cost to them.

Lightworkers are aware of something more than just the physical world. They will often believe in other realms, dimensions, spirits but also fae energy, and even other worldly. They do not need to be convinced of an afterlife or caught up in wanting scientific facts to believe in something. They can feel the vibrations of spirit around them; it is part of them within their own sacred heart. They simply live, breath, feel and sense it. It is a part of who they are and always has been. By carrying on the learnings, we can help to heal the world we live in and make a difference to welcoming a new world. Often lightworkers will respect the power of Mother Earth and all she holds dear to her. Let's face it the world we are currently in is a mess, Mother Earth is fighting more than ever before to reclaim her beauty. We all play a part in that whether we believe so or not.

I personally find it very ignorant whether you are governed by science or not, to think that we are the only evolved souls or life forms within, all the planets, all the stars, all the galaxies and universe. (Think about that for a moment... Earth is very small in where it sits within the solar system) ...

Before you fully commit to your own personal spiritual development, I want to share the following with you. This is something nobody ever really talked to me about, and I guess as a result I was quite naive about things when I started out, and sadly did get burned by people and situations along the way. Whilst I was given a sacred space to really explore and fully embrace my gift in, which I am forever grateful for. I also feel there were big gaps and discrepancies within my learnings, and to a degree I do feel at times I was let down by my mentors. Of course, there are lessons we have to go through, but a bit of advice I feel would have really prepared me for what was to come. This is the advice I wish to share with you that I feel I should have had some prior warning of...

The job of a lightworker is not easy and is not for the faint hearted. You may feel being spiritually awoken is all magic and fluffy unicorns! Sadly, it is not. When we fully commit to spirit it is a bit like signing a legal invisible documentation, there is no going back. You cannot suddenly unknown what you have learnt or been shown. I have known of some people that have started to develop, then got scared so have tried to shut down or close off. They end up becoming stuck and worse off than when they started out. Be sure within your own sacred heart you feel fully ready to embrace all the wonders spirit may have to show you, remember that where there is light there is also darkness.

You will find as you start to develop people around you will change. People you thought you knew and would be in your life forever, will suddenly see you in a different light. The gems in the crown will stay with you no matter what - be blessed to have these people. But be aware of others walking out of your world because your belief systems may be different to their own, and they may just not be able to comprehend this higher level of awareness. Family and friends sadly are not always loyal.

You will find you face endless ridicule and conflict within people's belief systems. Some may try and throw religion at you; others may tar you with the brush of doing the work of the devil. The truth of the matter is this is a projection of others ignorance and fear, this serves no place in your world. Do not ever feel you have to prove to anyone how you work with spirit. For you will have already been blessed by their power on some level, for the very fact you are here now reading this book...

Some people are too scared to tap into this ancient form of energy work, which has been around for thousands of years. It is my belief that through religion and conditioning systems we have lost a lot of the old ways. The old ways when everyone knew how to work with their own energy and power, in balance, peace and harmony. Some people prefer to stay asleep and keep the blindfold on. They are caught up in a materialistic world, often driven by ego and greed, be proud you are breaking free from the matrix system and have awoken to your own personal power and divine light.

You will find that as your level of spiritual awareness increases, and your vibration or frequency rises. Things will change around you. Things that may have once been important to you will no longer be. You will almost see the world in a new light, a new space. Enjoy this new realm that awaits you and embrace all the magick spirit wish to share.

By now you are probably starting to see that I am quite open and honest about things. With my own teachings I believe very much in keeping things real.

Remember to always trust... Not everyone that proclaims to work for the light is good. Energy doesn't lie, so if you feel a negative feeling about someone that on the face of things seems to be a good person, PAY ATTENTION... your psychic body is trying to pre-warn you. There is always a reason. It isn't always clear straight away, but energy has no reason to lie. The truth will always be exposed.

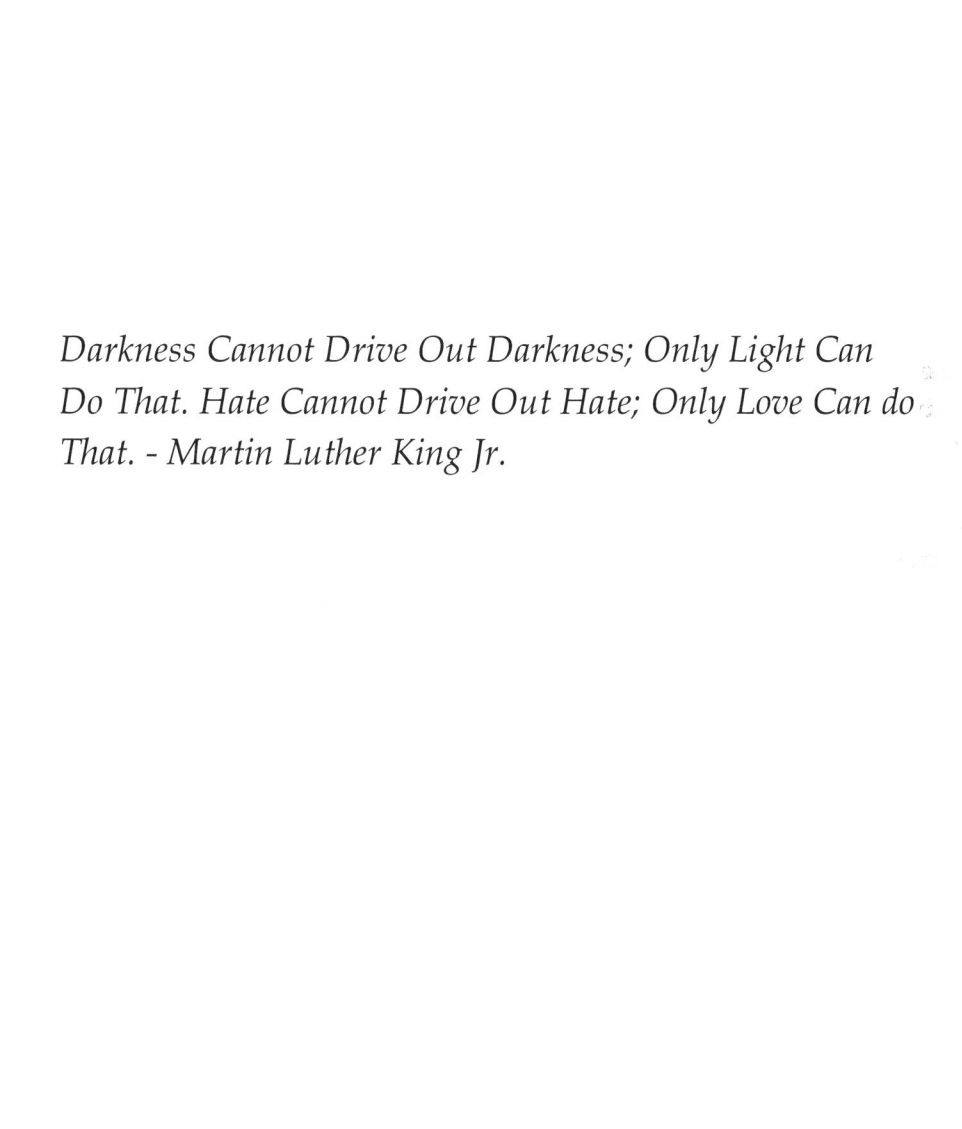

Darkness Cannot Drive Out Darkness; Only Light Can Do That. Hate Cannot Drive Out Hate; Only Love Can do That. - Martin Luther King Jr.

Your Spiritual Journal

Great! - you are still here reading, you are obviously ready to fully embrace your gift and own development journey... Development is a very complicated process, there are so many levels and layers and things to cover off and understand along the way. It is also a very personal experience and you will find some parts are easy to master, whilst other areas will challenge you.

What I would like for you to do at this stage is purchase yourself an A4 notebook. This can look as basic, or as colourful as you wish for it to be. This will become your **spiritual journal**. It's very important you are able to keep a record or documentation of your learnings. By doing this you will see as time goes on your own level of progression grows and increases, within this journal. Every time you do some form of psychic, mediumship or energy work, I would like you to make notes within this journal with a time and date, including what happened and how you found the experience to be good or bad.

(Please note - some people find this can be a hassle or a bit of an effort to undertake. If you take that attitude and approach, you may as well stop reading and close this book right now. Development is one of those things;

you get out what you put in. I cannot stress enough at this stage the importance of doing this. You will in time thank me and be grateful you had your spiritual journal. Fact - there is no fast track steps to development and if you try to shortcut the steps or learning, the only person that will get hurt, come unstuck and be affected by these actions will be <u>yourself</u>).

Invest the time needed for yourself now... By doing this you will be able to make your gift work best for you.

Trust

Perhaps of all the lessons and teachings within development, trust is by far the hardest and scariest thing to master and overcome. I wish I had a special tool or secret ingredient I could share with you, to make this lesson a little bit easier. But sadly, I do not. What I can however do is talk to you about the ways I have been able to tame and overcome the beast for the most part.

When we talk about trust it becomes scary because we naturally feel into the energy. Often, we don't have an object to put our trust into, it is just us. We are so worried <u>we</u> may mess up, or <u>we</u> may go wrong, <u>we</u> put a block or limitation on ourselves. But what is this block? It's merely a thought process or restriction and fear <u>we</u> have created; in truth it's a lie. What we have to start to do is remove ourselves from the situation... this takes time to master. But by removing yourself we become the channel or receiver of information. Whether you work psychically or mediumistically (you will learn more about this later).

In truth we actually put our trust in things on a daily basis that could fail us at any given time, go wrong, or let us down, yet we give it very little to no thought. The reason why... we have removed ourselves from the object or situation in question... There is no emotional feeling to the object therefore why doubt it?

- When we put a key in the door to lock or unlock our home. We don't think there could be a problem or issue (unless you know you have a dodgy door), we do this automatically. But every time we go to lock or unlock that door, there is a slim chance something could go wrong. The key could snap, the lock could break, and the key could become trapped or stuck. (Unless you are someone that may suffer with a form of OCD or panic attacks it's very unlikely you would give this a second thought.) There is no fear or limitation, or emotional connection attached with the object we are putting our trust into, therefore why doubt it?

- For those of us that have beautiful dogs. Every time before going on a walk with your dog, you may use a harness, or lead of some kind. You put your trust into these pieces of equipment. You trust that they will keep both your dog, you and other dog walkers and the general public safe. Yet at any time there is the reality and risk that the clasp on the harness could buckle or become undone. The lead could come loose or unclip or break, depending how much your dog may pull and tug. Putting extra strain and pressure on the equipment, causing your dog to become free and potentially putting them in great risk or danger. Yet we rarely give this thought. We go with the mindset and intention that all will be OK, and we trust that the harness and lead will not let us down.

- Perhaps one of the most used things we put our trust into, also has the most risks and power to go wrong and cause irreversible consequences is that of a car. Not all but most of us, at some stage in our life have put our trust into a car, whether we are the driver or just receiving a lift as a passenger. There is so much that could fail us. Both inside and outside with the car itself, the driver of the car, but also other road users that we have to come into contact with to get to our destination. Yet how many times do we get in and drive off with little to no thought that something will fail us or go wrong. Again, we go with the mindset and intention that all will be ok.

These are just a few examples of situations and things we put our trust into daily. If you stop and think about it, straight away you will think and know of many others, you could probably easily write a list of over a hundred others. The point is, however, we put our trust into all these things, with little to no thought, but at any time these things could fail us. Yet when it comes to putting the same level of trust into ourselves, we seem to really struggle to accept things for what they are. We look for a thousand reasons not to do something for fear of being judged, or making a mistake, yet how often do we feel confident in self to just trust and be? This largely goes back to the idea of conditioning. We have almost been brainwashed into giving away our power at every given opportunity, rather than standing tall within it.

The more you can stand and feel comfortable within your own power and energy field, the easier it will become to grow and develop your own gifts.

When I am working a public demonstration evening, I am often told after the demo... "You don't look nervous" or "You came across so confident". These things even now I struggle to accept and will often just smile to the people that have commented and move the conversation swiftly along. Whilst on the outside I may not look nervous I can hand on heart say inside I am shitting a brick. My stomach is often knotted with nerves and I am usually running back and forth to the toilet before the evening starts. There are some mediums I know that find these physical feelings too much to deal with, and although they are amazingly gifted, they do not work a public setting as these feelings are too much for them to go through. I have developed a few methods that have helped me through these times.

The first thing I have had to work on is that through all of these rollercoaster feelings of emotions spirit has my back. They are the ones pulling the strings at each and every stage when I work in a mediumship format. I have basically learnt to remove myself from my physical place or state of awareness to allow spirit in. (This takes time to do and the only advice I can give you is keep practicing).

When I was training and making sense of my own gift, this was something I was aware I was able to do a little more easily than some other members within the circle. The reason I feel this has been easier to achieve is that I was already doing this within my own body, long before I started to develop my own gifts.

I want to share with you a personal experience that might help give more understanding....

Throughout my middle school and college days I was bullied. My scars are not physical to see by the naked eye, but mental and emotional abuse. I sometimes used to wish it was just a quick scrap, or punch in the face as the bruises and wounds would heal quickly. We are not talking about a bit of abuse; we are talking about daily emotional abuse in nearly every class. On the way to and from school, and lunch breaks. It was like as soon as my feet passed my driveway to school the abuse would start, and there would be no let up until my feet touched my driveway and I was back on home soil. I often questioned the world around me, what had I done to deserve this? Constantly living on my nerves, and the experience sending me inside myself.

Often, I would spend school days in silence and would only speak when I needed to. I never ever cried; I had become completely immune to all the toxic venom that I had been subjected to. I knew that I was different, but I was OK with that and I never had a problem within myself. I was happy and proud of who I was, and even at an extremely young age I identified with myself as a witch, and a gay man. When I was subjected to the torture chamber of other people's spiteful thought patterns and words cast at me, it was a feeling of literally my spirit stepping out of its body. Not in the way of an out of body experience, but almost like the spirit stepping back.

The words would be fired at me, but they were just hitting a blank brick wall. I never ever challenged or reacted back. The poison literally just washed over me. I thought to myself 'Who are these people to spit this hateful venom at me? Who are you and what gives you any right or power to judge me? You actually know nothing about me or my world.' The more I stood in my own power, the more it annoyed the bullies; I made a commitment to myself that I would not be dragged down to the lower levels. For these hateful, toxic patterns where a reflection of somebody else's limitations, fears, and own insecurities, they served no place in my own world. I was acting as a mirror... It was not my truth.

What I have since learnt goes back once more to vibration. I was always vibrating on a higher frequency; I have never had an interest in causing hurt or pain intentionally to another. What is there to be gained by that? My sole focus in these darkest of times was art and photography. These subjects alone often kept me sane and alive. I would often be drawing away in silence, but really in thought I was having a good old conversation about everything and anything. (I have since come to learn I was connecting with my spirit guides and door keepers; you will learn more about these later).

I stayed completely authentic to myself; I did not buckle or cave into the demands of the bullies. I had often seen other victims do this and they then would be left alone. I was not prepared to inflict that level of hurt and coldness onto another for someone else's pleasure or personal gain. I am also aware this caused me to stay stuck and chained in the cycle of abuse for quite some years to follow. Until the day came, I was done with college, and unknown to any other at that time, I decided to free myself from the shackles of the education system and set myself free.

To go back to the subject of trust - I have had to trust in my spirit from an extremely young age. I would often ask in thought to be kept safe from any hurt and harm. Whilst I went through a lot of unneeded situations, at every stage I was indeed kept for the most part safe. I was working with my own intuition and already doing what a lot of development involves and is about, it never really left or went away, I just learnt its true title and meaning as time evolved within my world.

You must have mega trust with your spirit team when you undergo an evening of mediumship or deliver any message. You are in a room full of people, whilst on the face of it everyone is smiling and looking lovely, but below the surface lies an unheard energy, everyone has eyes on you, hoping, wanting, and praying a loved one with a message will come forward or be given for them. It can feel if you are not correctly protected, overwhelming and almost suffocating, you can feel the pressure and demand from the room to deliver the goods.

I always say the scariest part of mediumship is having no idea what will come out of my mouth until I stand up and connect. There are no pre-

prepared words or lines; you are literally putting your complete trust into an unseen energy. But every time I have sent the intentions and put my trust into the higher realms, they have always delivered the goods.

Trust Leads To Approachability And Open Communications - Scott Weiss

Ego

Before you can fully move forward with your own development journey we need to cover this subject matter. Be careful with this subject as ego has the power to swallow you up whole if you don't watch your step.

What is ego?

A person's sense of self-esteem or self-importance. 'Look what I am doing, how great I am, I am the greatest...' etc.

When developing your gift, the key thing to remember is the word <u>GIFT</u>. This is something that has been gifted to you from the higher realms of light. It is never something you personally have created or achieved. You have learnt how to make sense and use your gift to work with you. It's very much a partnership of energy.

Often within the spiritual scene lots of people trip up and drop the ball when it comes to ego. The moment you feel the information is coming from you personally as opposed to spirit, or psychic aura field energy there is a problem.

Be mindful that as you progress spirit are the teachers looking in, watching and overseeing all your actions. They have chosen you to represent all they stand for within the realm of light and love. You are their voice box, and work for them, should they feel you are misusing your gift, at any given stage no matter how advanced you may feel to be, spirit if they choose, can take your power away. They can disconnect you, and you will soon have egg on your face. Links will become broken and you would have a complete block within all areas of your energy work.

I have seen so many times mediums and psychics becoming far too cocky and arrogant, and dropping the ball before they have even started out. Stay grounded and humble. Be sure to regularly scan your body and behaviour. If you see you are starting to become consumed in ego step back and look from the higher perspective, if there is a pattern emerging you don't like - fix it quickly.

When we develop there is naturally some ego in us all. We all get very excited when we first start out and can channel a message from spirit for someone and the receiver can make sense of all you have said. Of course, it's important to celebrate this, as it shows your links with your spirit team are becoming stronger, and you are gaining trust and confidence with them. But be mindful it is your spirit team doing the work, and not you personally. There is a fine line between celebrating something and feeling confident, but don't allow that to consume you into the place of, 'look what I can do it's all about me me me'.

I find it very awkward when people recommend the work that I do. Quite often I will receive messages from people enquiring about readings and the message will include something like "You have come highly recommended" or "My friend saw you and said you were amazing," or "I've heard you are the best in the area and can deliver the goods". When I read these types of messages straight away I feel a tightness in my chest and a sense of panic, this puts me off wanting to even see this person if I'm being honest. Whilst it's lovely they have faith in the work I do. I am constantly aware it's only what spirit is allowing me to bring forward from their power direct. There is absolutely no guarantee I can personally bring through the person they want to connect with, or anyone for that matter, and you will never hear me make such a claim.

Each reading is always classed as an experiment only. Sadly, something I have noticed is when you work in the public eye, people try to transfer an unrealistic amount of their own demands on what they feel you can actually do. You will notice these may be the claims you hear from other people, but <u>NEVER</u> from me direct.

When you go to a spiritual or psychic fayre, you will see there are lots of posters and banners to advertise a person's work. Often you will notice bold headers and titles with sometimes quite big statements, including things like... 'Britain's Best Loved Medium' or 'Number One Psychic' or 'Do You Dare To Be Amazed' or 'One Hundred Percent Accurate Readings Available' etc... (Please note these are not aimed at anyone in particular just a common theme).

If you have ever noticed my posters or banner it will simply say my name 'Mitch Garlington' then below... 'Spiritual Medium - Psychic - Tarot Reader'. I simply state the style and ways I work. That is all no fancy slogans, no exaggerated claims. As the truth is no matter how much I would love to be right all the time that is unrealistic. There are times as I have stated earlier in the book, no matter how much I try to connect with a loved one, if they do not want to step forward, I cannot force them or 'click' them in. Be mindful of what you are proclaiming you can and cannot do. The best advice is to allow spirit to do the work, and let the <u>evidence</u> speak for itself.

I had an experience that left me questioning the people that come for readings, and the demands they often have not that long ago.

I had seen a lovely female client on and off throughout the year of 2017. Her readings with me were sometimes online, and when I was in her area face to face. Over a period of a year she had had around five readings with me in total and was always left impressed. In early 2018 she booked a reading online, I worked with my spirit team in the normal way and used the tarot as guidance as I always do. To my horror she was extremely upset, angry and disappointed with her reading. She started to challenge each card and said the reading made absolutely no sense. She even went on to presume I had not taken the correct steps to conduct my reading beforehand.

For those that know me well you will know, I take all aspects of my spiritual work extremely seriously. I never cut corners or become lapse where protection and rituals are concerned (you will learn more about these later). I simply apologised to the client but explained the cards came out from her energy for a reason, the messages from spirit were channeled from her energy, for a reason.

I made it clear I was only the telephone mouthpiece and receiver of information. I feel the real underlying issue she had was she was cross that an area of her world hadn't been mentioned or talked about, as she became very nasty towards me because I had not brought this up. What she failed to understand or want to acknowledge was that her own actions were blocking this certain subject. The cards were wanting her to look at these other areas or points within her world, by correcting those, she would have removed the block around this other situation.

Despite trying to talk through the reading and reassure her, she made the decision at that point that I was clearly a fraud, a cold reader, and full of bullshit. (Despite me having given her five previous readings that in her own words were 'spot on'). She made the decision to unsubscribe from all my various social media and informed me she would never book with me again. She also became extremely hostile when I said I wouldn't read for her again. I will treat everyone as equal but... as soon as someone throws abuse or makes claims that are untrue; the exchange of energy needed to read for a client has become broken and is no longer there. I sent her energy away with love.

The sad matter was that she had placed in her own thoughts, an unrealistic expectation of what she felt I was able to do. The ego within me almost wanted to shout and scream back, I was hurt and upset by the experience. But I also knew that this energy served no point to me personally and would end up giving me more hurt if I didn't disconnect from it. I had to embrace this for what it was and draw a line in the sand.

Thankfully this has been the only time something of that nature has happened. This was also a lesson and learning for me. No matter how many times you read for someone, through no fault of your own however genuine and pure your intentions are, other people's ego can play a large role in the experience of a reading. Sadly, not all people are loyal. To have had five perfect readings with me, but to disregard all areas of my work based on one, in her view, negative reading was a complete shock and eye-opening experience. All you can do in these situations is remain thankful in your heart and thank your spirit team for the learning and lesson that was gifted however challenging it might have felt at the time.

Always remember the reason you are using your gift - for the greater good, to allow a person to heal, to give hope and reassurance that life goes on after we leave this earthly realm, to show that the greatest power we all hold within our heart is the gift of unconditional love. We are not here to walk for or take away life lessons for others. We can highlight something or make a person aware, but we all hold the power of free will. If a person is not ready to see or chooses to overlook something that has been pre-warned of, as a reader you can do no more.

I don't want you to be reading this book and thinking, 'oh my, Mitch you must be perfect'. I am flawed like we all are, otherwise, I wouldn't be on Earth learning the lessons I still have to learn, as well as sharing and passing the knowledge on, I make mistakes and mess up on a regular basis just like a lot of us.

I want to share with you another experience I had when I was completely consumed by ego and arrogance. This was a time before my spirit work began. Whilst I didn't realise at the time this was part of my shadow side, and negative things I had to heal. I have talked about this quite a lot in my second book 'Stranger In This World', but the experience carried with it several lessons that I believe have stood me in good stead where my own mediumship and spiritually work are concerned.

Before I really embraced my gift, I worked in an aggressive sales and advertising company. This was a world fuelled by ego, materialism and greed. I was in this world every day, for forty hours, five days a week, so to a degree you become consumed and it takes over without you fully recognising or being aware. Often there would be a battle of the egos for who could be top salesperson or achieve the highest amount of commission. Ego was fuelled, flared and rubbed up and down daily.

I also had a part time career as a Cher drag queen impersonator. Was I a good impersonator? The truth is yes and no... I was good at doing the makeup and costumes and creating the theatre and show. But I guess looking back now I thought really, I was a little untouchable. I used to mime a lot of the show, but sometimes it was requested by venues to sing live. Being a drag queen, I learnt very quickly you can get away with a lot more than a standard tribute show. I wasn't the worst at singing, but Cher I definitely was not. I used to blag my way through the singing parts and by adding a bit of humour I got away with it.

Truth was I was trying to shortcut and fast track my progression. I was hungry for the spotlight, I loved the attention and the audience reaction to drag, I suppose it gave me a bit of a buzz and adrenaline rush, I was also using it as a distraction to mask my own depression at that period. It almost became addictive and the more I did it, the more I needed a regular fix.

Lots of drag artists are inspired by the power of Cher. I have many friends in the business that also impersonated her. Often, they didn't have the high paid job I was in and so the costumes would be homemade, a little more basic and quite often looked cheap, rough and of poor quality. Because I had a good job, I would spend hundreds and nearly thousands of pounds to have the best. The reality was with these other performers, they all had proper talent and they could all sing and hold a tune - the one chink in my armour.

A bit like within the spiritual scene impersonators and tribute shows advertise a lot! I quickly had posters made up proclaiming I was... 'The UK's Number One Cher Extravaganza Tribute Drag Show'. Wow, just saying that now is a very bold statement!

Did I believe, I was better than all these other impersonators? Well the truth was at that time yes and no... As far as the look and costumes where concerned yes, I felt I had the edge. But actual talent - no. However, I used smoke and mirrors to mask that small technicality.

This behaviour was always going to be short lived and come at a cost. I was also awakening to my spiritual potential, spirit had tried to work with me before but failed, and I think they were becoming impatient. I did a show in Worthing that really looking back now there were huge warning signs. I do believe this was in some ways a test from spirit, certainly a lesson I would carry with me forever more. This is really where my own ego got the better of me. The psychic in me could feel the energy of the place was wrong on all levels, and I just didn't have a good feeling.

The performer and drag diva in me knew the show had to go on, and so it did but ultimately at a cost! The show started and all was going well, but around four songs in I went backstage for a costume change. There was an instrumental section within the backing track, giving me about three to four minutes for a complete fast change.

Whilst I was mid costume change the backing track stopped, and the owner of the venue demanded I come out on stage. I received the biggest dressing down of my life! In front of a pub full of people, and at that moment in time my world became shattered. I remember the words clearly, "your set is lovely, your costumes are amazing, you look spot on, but darling... you cannot sing - you have no real talent". I was told to take a good long look in the mirror and have a chat with myself on what it was I was good at doing, as a singer I was not.

I endured the wrath of the audience and it has been one of the hardest, most embarrassing things to have had happen to me. But also, it was the best gift I could have ever been given. It was like a harsh, hard, reality slap in the face, and this experience allowed me to embrace my true spiritual gifts within.

I talked in the previous chapter about trust. The above experience also has played a part in trusting my spirit team. When I am riddled with nerves before I stand up or go on to do a demo. I often say in thought to myself 'Whatever happens, even if I am only able to channel one message. It won't be as bad as the time I was booed off stage in Worthing dressed in full Cher drag'. This thought usually makes me laugh on some level and gives me the needed confidence, to stand up and just be guided by spirit.

The truth is nerves are an important part of our spiritual journey; they help to keep us balanced and grounded. They remind us that we are working from the heart. If we went in with no nerves, feeling we were the best in the business and a cut above the rest. Are we really working from the higher realms of light? Or merely from our own place of ego?

When I performed as Cher, I very rarely felt nervous. In short, I was working from ego...

When I stand up to work with spirit, whilst it might not be viewable from the naked eye. My body is shaking inside and out with nerves...

The day I stop being nervous with my own spiritual gifts, is the day I have dropped the ball...

Remember FEAR is also a gift and does one of two things...

Forget Everything And Run ... or... Face Everything And Rise

More The Knowledge Lesser The Ego, Lesser The Knowledge More The Ego... - Albert Einstein

Breaking Free from the Matrix System

You may start to feel the world around you changing as you start to strengthen your gifts. You will start to notice things that were once important to you, may become irrelevant. Depending how quickly or slowly your personal development journey takes, you may start to feel a bit lost or isolated within the world you once knew. As and when this happens our outlook and perspective on life starts to change. Developing awareness is not just within the spirit world, it also opens our eyes to the physical place we are in. For those of you that are particularly empathic, you may find these feelings become overwhelming for a time. Know and trust it is completely natural and a normal part of self-development.

It is often known as breaking free from the matrix system. But what does this actually mean?

I talked earlier in the book about being conditioned. From the moment we are born and enter this world this process starts on some level to happen. We start to become brought up in whatever world we find ourselves in and the demands and expectations are placed upon us accordingly.

To be conditioned means we must live and abide by a pre-set structure of rules and regulations, or thoughts and ideas. This is all well and good and can protect us and keep us safe to a degree. But what happens when we learn the truth of these rules and regulations, or thoughts and ideas? What I mean by that is often the rules can twist and bend, or parts of the information have been altered and changed en route, so in some ways we are being set up to fail from the off and lied to...

Religion has always played a huge part in this world. Whilst I was christened, I have no religious faith from within, and I do not identify with the Christian religion on any level. From as far back as I can remember I identified myself as a male witch. Yet when I went to school this was something never spoken about or really acknowledged. In religious education we learnt about many faiths from Christianity, Catholic, Buddhism and so on. But at no stage was I taught about the ways of the traditional witch or pagan following. But why?

These followings of the old ways, where pre-religion. A time when everyone worked in peace, harmony with love and magick in their heart. Religion has brought in fear and an order of importance or system into the world. In many religions today to be a witch you are tarred with the brush of doing the devil's work. There is so much ignorance and hostility, yet very few people even in today's times still understand the true meaning or definition of the word.

Witch - the true meaning is often associated with a female, but in truth can also be male. They are a healer and work with the treasures of the earth, to aid in natural healing remedy and cure. They work with the seen and unseen world. They are often a channel for spirit and psychic awareness.

In today's world there are many styles and forms of witchcraft. Whilst there is a huge diversity the end goal is usually the same. Religion through the ages has abused the word witchcraft, often feeding it to be something of the dark arts. Religion has been able to misguide people through fear, and by doing so the blood of so many innocents has been spilt, all in the name of a higher power or god. But ask yourself would God really seek to slaughter so many, when all a witch is doing is providing a sacred space for a person to heal and be themselves?

This is just one example and there are many, many more...

Take Christmas for example, when we are young most of us are taught to believe in Santa or Father Christmas. It's not until we become older, we learn the truth, of our blessed Mum or Dad keeping the secret and tradition alive for as long as they feel is right to do so. Often, we feel a mix of emotions, we knew it was them on the one hand and laugh it off. But part of us feels a bit disappointed we have been lied to for all those years and been conditioned into thinking this was real.

But where does Christmas really come from? The true meaning again stems back to the old ways and is in fact a pagan festival to honour winter solstice. It was only when Christianity faith came about that these festivals became, altered, tweaked, forgotten and changed. Once more showing the power of what the conditioning system can do.

We can look at this from a whole different perspective as it goes far beyond just religion. Often people approach me to do charity demo evenings. When and where possible I will always give my time up freely to help charities. But as time goes on, I am becoming increasingly selective with what I choose to help in. You may ask yourself why and think that to help any charity is worth doing, and of course to a degree it is. But with the new world we are living in, people are starting to take the blindfold off and see the world of conditioning for what it really is.

Let's take <u>some</u> cancer charities for example. In recent years people are becoming aware that cannabis is able to dramatically reduce and, in some situations, even stop, slow down and cure the condition of cancer. Yet this information has been hidden from public domain for years. The information isn't new, it has literally been hidden from our day to day world. When people in the past have tried to awake the masses and informed them of this idea to be true, they have not believed, and have often laughed and written these ideas off. The question is 'who has kept this important information from the world we live in?' We are learning ever more that natural medicine has the power to restore the body's health.

This then makes me ask the question... all the money raised by some of the big top cancer charities, daily, where is that money going? And what is it really being spent on? Hundreds and thousands of pounds are raised and donated daily?

The sad fact of the world we live in today is that more than 70% of the foods and certain drinks we have, aid in cancer growth. With the level or research these charities proclaim they do, why are we still allowing these things to go into our food and drink like it's normal? This is a sadly a fact. Big drug companies get big money from people being ill and to realise and reveal a cure would cease and stop their funding. (You may or may not agree with this statement, and that is of course OK as you have your own freedom or freewill).

Sadly, like many of us I have lost dear friends, and loved ones to this toxic disease. But I also have had many friends that have made the decision, to fight their battle and take a stand with cannabis and other alternative remedies and treatments. In these situations and experiences more people have survived and cured themselves than not. I think cancer charities certainly can help people, and some do amazingly valuable work. But... in equal measure, to not ask the question and challenge back where is all this money really going? Is quite naive...

I spoke about only helping select charities, for me personally I would rather support a local charity or 'go fund me' page. The real everyday people that are trying to survive and make a better world for themselves. Often, they get overlooked through the demands of the big cats. People think because they have donated to a big-name charity, they have done well. Of course, the intention is indeed good and genuine, but the reality is that their money has probably been misused to line someone else's pocket, and not aided in the charity's goal.

It doesn't just end there...

There are many other examples I could share with you.

Let's take tax for example. For those of us that work we are all required to pay a level of income tax. Often the little independent man gets stung the most with this. Whilst the big highflyers and top earners seem to find endless loopholes to get out of paying.

Let's look at Parliament, how often do we hear of misuse of tax returns? Claiming for big houses, fancy holidays and more, and putting this through as business expenses? Whilst some of these abusers do get pulled up, there are far more continuing to misuse the system. The system itself works and has a place or purpose, but through peoples' own behaviour and allowing the rules and structure to be twisted and manipulated, you are set up to fail before you have begun.

These are quite big examples of how the world we live in has become full of broken promises and structure betrayal.

You will probably start to see levels of this within your own everyday world. Something that always stands out for me was when I was working at a high-end bed retailer. There was a structure and process in place all staff had to follow. Yet often the ego hungry, top salespeople within the business would bend and really manipulate the rules for personal gain.

Now in theory those people should have been pulled up and dealt with, but often their own sales targets laced the higher up bosses' wage packets. So instead of following the rules and required actions, often these very people would be celebrated, yet their own behaviour was completely untrustworthy and ethically wrong. Once more showing that the system that everyone should be following was broken, it was not a fair starting point. Why should someone exceeding their targets get away with misuse, as opposed to someone not hitting target but following the rules and structure?

In my own journey of awakening this was the point that I started to wake up, and really see the world in its true ugliest form. The rose-tinted glasses had truly fallen off.

This is the main thing to remember when you awake to the true reality of what is going on in front you, you cannot suddenly un-see what you have been shown.

I would often try and talk about these subjects to other people that I worked with. The very fact I even challenged some of these ideas was very taboo... People often looked at me as if I was fresh out of the mad house! and that my ideas where complete nonsense. The reality was these people did not want and were not ready to see beyond the end of their own nose and their bubble. It's far easier to stay consumed and asleep in a broken conditioning system, than have the bravery to stand up and walk away from something that is in effect garbage.

I didn't care how much money I earned in commission, or if I was the top salesperson in the south west at my company. Outside of that employer those things meant nothing and were worthless. They were the rules to abide by in company time, but I knew in equal measure these would serve no purpose in my world moving forward. The world can be as dark or as light as we choose to see it in.

When I decided to truly follow my spiritual calling, it was to always work for the divine light. I knew that the work I would go on to do, would be a starting point to allow people the space to heal and just be the best version of themselves. From the messages and feedback I receive from clients, I know that the work spirit allow me to do is helping and saving people on a daily basis. This is worth far more than what money can buy. I will never be as rich as I once was with material wealth, but I am already richer than I have ever been before since following my calling.

When you feel ready to fully break free from the matrix system, that's when the wonders of the universe can be revealed to you.

When you first start to unplug or disconnect from the matrix system, you will feel waves of emotions. You will feel a sense of power and awaken within your heart centre. You may also feel some sorrow or guilt. This is a very powerful stage of development as you are choosing to make a stand for a better world. Your actions are showing to the world boundaries…all that you are willing to accept and all that must go.

Breaking free from the restraints takes bravery, stand tall and be proud you have awoken from this slumber.

"The Matrix Is Everywhere. It Is All Around Us. Even Now, In This Very Room. You can See It When You Look Out Your Window, Or When You Turn On Your Television. You can Feel It When You Go To Work, When You Go To church, When You Pay your Taxes. It Is The World That Has Been Pulled Over Your Eyes To Blind You From The Truth. You Are A Slave. Like Everyone Else You Were Born Into Bondage, Born Into A Prison That You Cannot Smell Or Taste Or Touch. A Prison For Your Mind". - Morpheus - The Matrix

Sitting Within the Power

This is really the space and area you need to focus on the most with any form of self-development journey. But you would be surprised how many people don't give themselves the opportunity to sit within the power, or they try to fast track or shortcut this process?

What does sitting in the power mean?

It's literally giving you time daily to sit and be still. Allowing your mind, body and spirit the freedom to just be at peace with each other. Finding a sacred space either within your home or somewhere you can freely be to do this, a place that's personal for you where you won't be disturbed.

Before you can understand the thoughts, feelings, and actions of the spirit world, and what they want to link, say, and pass on. You must first understand your own energy, your own thoughts, feelings, actions and desires. This is key to developing psychic and mediumship ability. You must be able to know and trust the thoughts and feelings that are your own, and those of which you are connecting with spiritually.

Exercise – Sitting within the Power

What I would like you to do is give yourself a minimum of ten minutes per day (more if you are able to) where you sit within your own power. This may be of a morning, after lunch, or more of an afternoon or evening activity. The freedom and choices are endless. Set an alarm so you can give yourself the needed amount of time.

What I want you to do is set aside this time daily and just sit and be. You can choose if you would like gentle instrumental music on in the background or you may prefer to sit in the quiet.

Sitting in the power is a form of meditation. This helps us to make sense of the place and space you are in right now. It also allows your physical body the chance to rest and just be still. What you will find happens for the first couple of weeks to a month is, you will use this space to process. Your thoughts will start off very busy to begin with, but that is OK and what you are allowing your mind to do is space clear.

Many people feel when you meditate you should be in a deep trance, spaced out Zen state. Whilst this can happen, it's not so much about being 'zenned' out. It's more important to be able to process, slow down, quieten and in time silence the white nose that might be inside your head. Think of it like a computer defragmenting.

Journal prompt - each time you do this activity, I would like you to make notes in your spiritual journal with a date and time. Write down anything you felt good or bad and key points you took from the experience.

What will start to happen is you will be challenged with an array of emotions. Things from your past may in time come to the surface to be explored. When we meditate quite often, we don't just rest and relax it can also be a form of healing and clearing.

You may find as you adapt to this process some days you get lots from it, other days not very much. But be consistent with it, as ultimately this will be the key to success and long-term progression moving forward. By making notes in your journal you will be able to look over and see the forward movement in your progress.

As time goes on you will start to identify on a deeper level, the way you process and digest information. As you develop your gifts you may start to notice in time thoughts and feelings, visualisations or insights start to come to you from a slightly different space. When this happens, this is known as channeling, and you are starting to channel the energy from the spirit world. It may at first seem confusing and not always make much sense. This is why keeping the spiritual journal is very important to record as and when that power starts to amplify for you.

As times goes on within this book, we will be able to do deeper exercises around this area of work. But for now, understanding your own energy is where we need to be.

Remember sitting in the power like all areas of self-development is a personal journey and experience. Don't worry so much about if you are doing it right or wrong. Trust the process and you cannot go wrong. Just allow yourself the space to go with the flow. You may decide for you, you get better results out within nature - a garden, a field, a wood or by the sea, or you may be quite happy just connecting sitting on your bed. Whatever works best for you is fine. Don't be scared to try different ways until you find what you're most comfortable with. For some people they also may hold a crystal of choice within their hand. Or they may just allow their hands to rest within their lap; again, whatever you find most comfortable will be the correct way for you.

Most importantly enjoy the freedom and power of connecting with the core spirit of who you truly are. You will start to understand your true identity and see yourself in a new light.

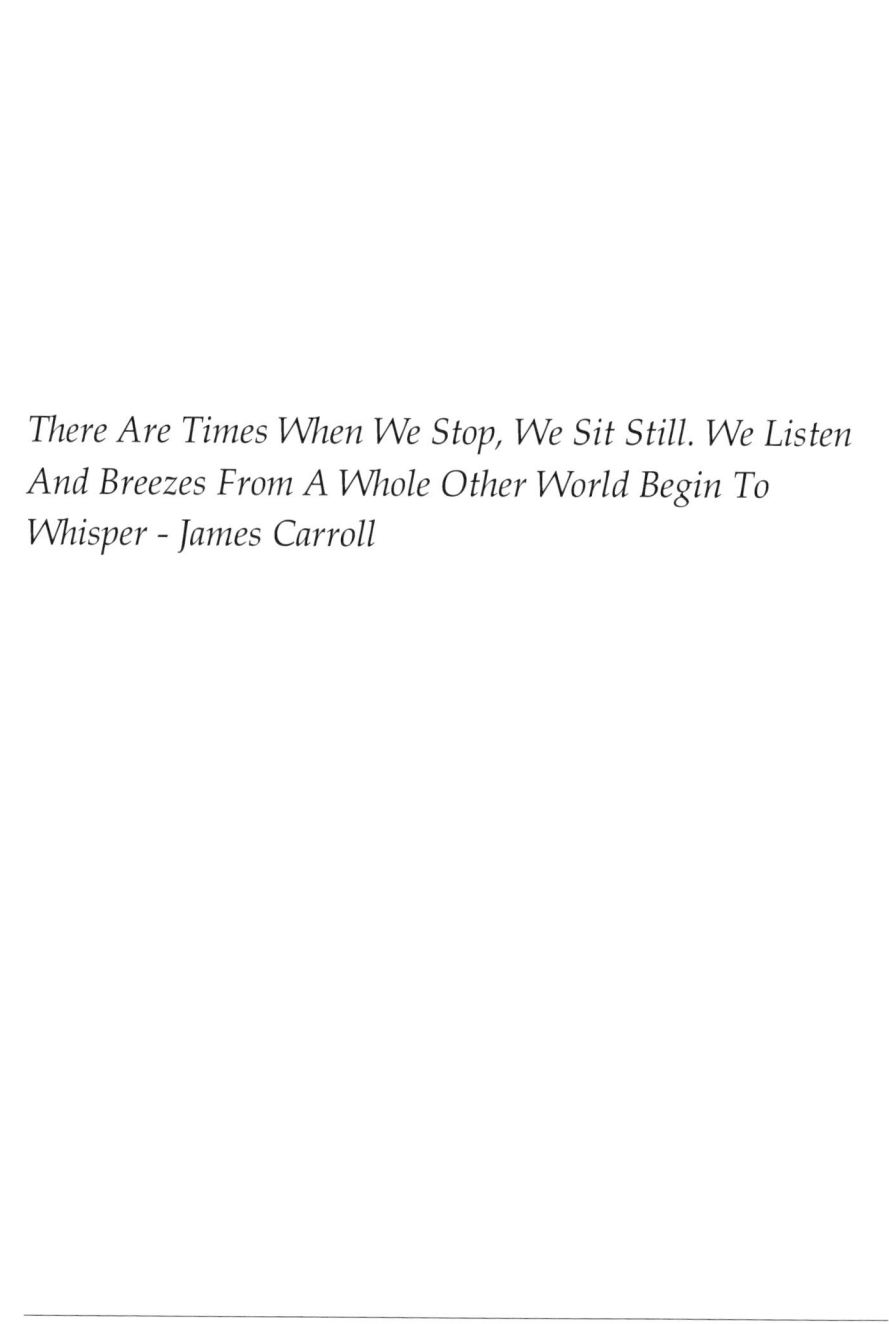

There Are Times When We Stop, We Sit Still. We Listen And Breezes From A Whole Other World Begin To Whisper - James Carroll

Energy

This subject matter itself is very complex but something we need to make sense of, when we work psychically or spiritually, we are linking in with various energies. The following topic has been broken down into sections to try and make it easier to understand and digest...

What is energy?

As I mentioned early in the book everything in this world has and holds an energy or vibration of its own. From the floor beneath your feet, to the glass of drink you hold in your hand, to the animal or pet that might be in the room with you right now.

Energy is a form of Breath of life.

When we breathe, we can see and feel the breath of life. Because we can see it and sense it, we don't need to question it, we accept it's there and take it for what it is.

But... some energies cannot be seen in the same way but felt or sensed. I would like to share with you an exercise to feel and understand energy...

Exercise – Energy

Place your hands together palm to palm. Just spend a few moments with both hands touching each other. Your hands may feel hot or cold and that is fine. Now gentle start to move them apart, leaving a distance of about four to five centimetres. You will start to feel that there is an energy ball within the centre palms of your hands. Now everyone feels and senses energy differently, you may feel it like a magnet almost bouncing from each palm. Or you may see it as a smoky mist or possible colour, or you may get some other sensation...

Now gently spread your hands a little further and you will feel the energy becoming stronger and the ball growing bigger. Depending on how you move your hands you will find you can manipulate and play around with this energy ball. For those that can send healing this is often a way in which we can send distant healing. You can think of someone who may need some healing energy and love at this time, and just send this ball to them in your thoughts. When the ball is released you will feel the energy leaving and disbursing from your hands.

Journal prompt - (If you find at first you cannot feel anything spend a little longer practicing this exercise - make notes in your spiritual journal on how you found this experience to be).

How else can we feel energy?

This is something that we naturally tap into daily, yet often overlook or take for granted. How often have you walked into a room and before you have even greeted anyone or opened your mouth, you have sensed or picked up there is an atmosphere? This may be positive or negative depending on the situation. Then in return how has that energy affected you? If it's been positive most likely it has made you feel happy, upbeat, or possibly caused you to laugh. It would have certainly made you feel good and you probably stayed in the room for a length of time, with a smile on your face.

But...

What about if the energy felt negative? You may have sensed there was an awkwardness or uncomfortable feeling? It may have made you feel angry, sad, hostile or even emotional? It would have made you feel uncomfortable and you probably felt like you needed to leave the room as quickly as possible. We can all feel energy on some level. When we work with energy in a spiritual way, as well as the obvious feelings we work even deeper with the energy lines around us. When we start to work in this way, we are tapping into the aura field and chakra system.

Whilst I am not big on science it does have and hold its place within the spiritual world and has its importance. A word of caution - this next section of the book is going to explore some of the science that we need to be aware of, that will work hand in hand with our spiritual growth...

Aura Field

What is an Aura Field?

The aura field is the energy that we see around a person, or a plant, animal or even an object. As everything is energy it also has its own aura field. When we work in a spiritual way, we use the aura field to aid our psychic and mediumship ability.

The human aura...

The human aura is an energy field that surrounds the human body and reflects the subtle life energies that work within and around it. It is made up of seven layers; imagine seven layers of electrical current that are around us. They can at times be seen when they need to be but are not always easy to see at first with the naked eye. This is similar to the magnetic field that surrounds a simple magnet. Like a magnetic field, the aura is generated within physical matter - but is also greatly affected by its surroundings.

The energies flowing through the aura make us what we are and are in turn affected by our surrounding life conditions and the lifestyle we choose to lead.

The aura reflects the activity of our organs, health, mental activity and emotional state. It can also show or highlight disease - often long before the development of physical symptoms. The strength and properties of an aura are determined by the amount, and quality of, the energies flowing through it.

The human aura is made up of the following seven layers (the diagram below gives more insight into how the layers look)

- **Casual Body** - Mental Aspect

- **Celestial Body** - Emotional Aspect

- **Etheric Template** - Higher Physical Aspect

- **Astral Body**

- **Mental Body** - Lower Mental Aspect

- **Emotional Body** - Lower Emotional Aspect

- **Etheric Body** - Lower Aspect

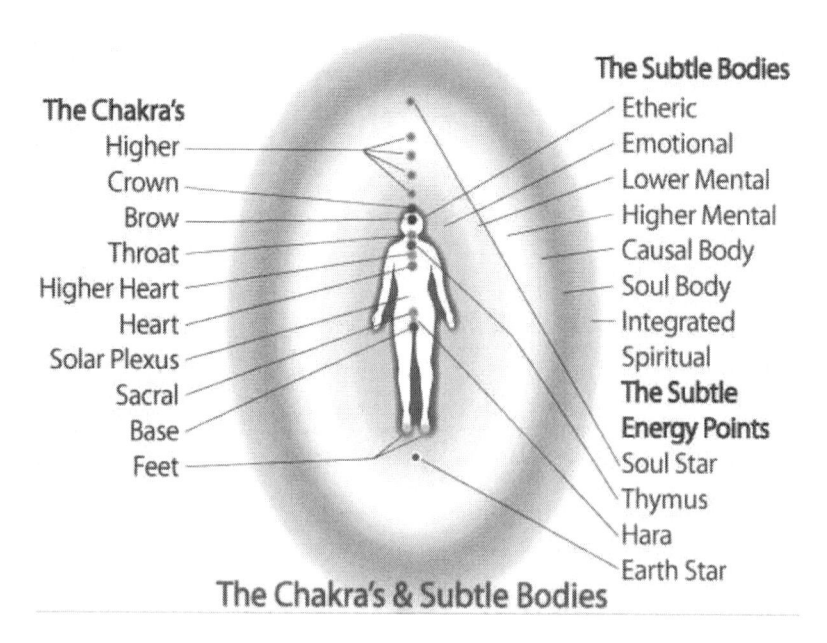

The Chakra's
Higher
Crown
Brow
Throat
Higher Heart
Heart
Solar Plexus
Sacral
Base
Feet

The Subtle Bodies
Etheric
Emotional
Lower Mental
Higher Mental
Causal Body
Soul Body
Integrated
Spiritual

The Subtle Energy Points
Soul Star
Thymus
Hara
Earth Star

The Chakra's & Subtle Bodies

The chakra system also plays a huge part with what is happening internally, but we will look at this a little later. The main aura is banded around the body. As you can see from the diagram, it is like thick, coloured hoops of light that surround a person's body that are almost egg-shaped. The main colours of the aura emanate from the primary energy centres - the major chakra system - (we will look more at this shortly). The individual bands of colour are difficult to see, unless you have a very well-developed auric sight. People that have developed a strong auric sight will often say they can see a haze or colour around a person. When this happens, they are seeing a layer of an aura.

Aura photography, or to give it the correct name Kirlian photography, is an experience that I would encourage you to investigate at least once. This is where you can have your aura photographed. The photographer will usually go into detail with what has been picked up and any recommendations needed to make the aura stronger, cleaner or healthier, if there are any issues picked up.

I try and have my aura photograph done a couple of times a year. Imagine if you were a car owner, it's a bit like getting a service done. Very often we focus on the physical side of life, health, diet, etc. but often overlook what's going on in the aura field - the very place that can tell us a lot more about our body and bodies. By becoming more aware and in tune with our own aura, not only do we develop a deeper understanding of who we are and our core spirit and authentic soul, we can also take more care of ourselves, in return leading a better quality of life.

The Etheric Aura...

Close to the skin is the etheric aura. This is often known as 'The Vitality Sheath'. It can be seen with the naked eye, as a pale, narrow band, next to the skin, outlining the body. This is usually no more than half an inch wide depending on the vitality of a person. It looks like a dense layer of pale smoke, gently around or on the skin. This is the visible part of the energy body, in its contracted state.

During sleep, the etheric aura expands and opens becoming larger and finer in order to absorb and store vital cosmic energy within it. After sleep, the energy body contracts and forms a dense sheath surrounding the body, close to the skin. This holds within it the stored energies we all need for living. In a way, the energy body is like a living storage battery. During sleep, it automatically sets itself on recharge, replacing the energies that have been used up.

The aura is a device through which you create your own experience of reality, of health, emotions, mind and spirituality. It is a major energy field which surrounds the human body. There are seven major auric layers, known at this time. There is an interdependent relationship between your auric layers and the seven major chakras of the body which we will explore shortly.

Now we are starting to get an understanding of how the aura works, it's time to go a little deeper and look at each of the seven layers in more depth...

The Etheric layer - This layer lies close to the human body approximately half an inch wide (1.3 centimetres). It is usually grey, white or blue in colour. Its vibrancy indicates strong or weak health. It is primarily connected to the base chakra known as the life force. It is the most easily seen auric layer or etheric field. This field can also be seen around trees, plants, animals and even inanimate objects such as furniture. A white or black background will often highlight the etheric field.

The Emotional Body - This layer lies beyond the etheric field and extends to one of three inches (8 centimetres). It is strongly connected to the pelvic chakra. It contains, when healthy, beautiful, bright orbs of energy and colour. These primary colours are emitted as the emotions change.

The Mental Body - This layer lies beyond the emotional body and is composed of clear yellow, green or blue colours when healthy. It indicates the thoughts and attitudes of the person. It is connected to the solar plexus chakra and extends three to eight inches (19 centimetres) out from the body.

The Astral Body - This layer lies beyond the mental body and is closely connected to the heart chakra. It is full of beautiful pastel colours such as pinks, greens and blues when healthy and unblocked. It extends up to one foot (30 centimetres) from the body and indicates your capacity for conditional and unconditional love.

The Etheric Template - This layer lies beyond the astral body field and is a type of x-ray or blueprint of the physical body. Illness or blocks can be observed and treated in this field and this is relayed to the physical body. It extends one to two feet (60 centimetres) from the body. This layer is connected to the throat chakra. It is usually observed as grey, blue in colour.

The Celestial Body - This layer is the sixth auric field and extends two to three feet (90 centimetres) from the body. It is connected to the third eye chakra and is filled with mother of pearl colours and energies. It is the layer through which you can experience spiritual ecstasy.

The Casual Body - This layer also known as the Ketheric template is connected to the crown chakra and is a type of photographic negative of the mental and spiritual aspects of a person. It is usually filled with golden shimmering light and is surrounded by a gold or silver halo or outer rim of protection. It extends from three to four feet (130 centimetres) outwards from the person.

Now we know some of the science behind the aura. As your development progresses you may find in time you start to see the colours a little easier. Below is a breakdown of the main colours you may come into contact with and their meanings. Aura colours change depending on your health, mood, spiritual state of being and more. The most common colours seen around people are the following....

Pink - Love, Femininity, Unconditional love, Pregnancy

Maroon - Life Work, Vocation, Ambition

Dark Red - Anger, Hate, Violence, Passion

Bright Red - Passion, Life Energy, Vitality

Orange - Ambition, Vitality, creativity, Artistic

Orange/Red - Sexuality, Energy

Yellow - Joy, Purity, Happiness, Optimistic

Green - Intellect, Nature connection, Interest

Dirty Green - Envy, Spite, Illness, Jealousy

Blue - Teacher, Spiritual Feelings, Higher connection

Purple - Ideas, Deep Spiritual Awakening

Grey - Depression, Tiredness, Illness, Addictions, Lack Of Sleep Or Spiritual Oneness

Black - Extreme Illness, Disease, Addictions, Near Death

Silver - Strong connection To The Divine, Angels, Unconditional Love, Teacher

Gold - Divine Light, Purity, Enlighten

Now you have some understanding of how the aura works and what the colours mean and represent.

I am very much a believer in keeping development as simple as possible. If the aura is an area you want to explore and research in more depth and detail, there are many fantastic books out there which go into great scientific details and understandings. I would always encourage you to do ongoing research should you feel guided to do so.

The Chakra System and the Seven Major Chakras

It is now time to look and what is happening internally within the body and understand the power of the chakra system. Within our bodies we have thousands of mini or minor chakras known as meridian energy points. The word chakra means spinning wheel, and the body is made up of thousands of energy points that are in a constant state of rotation or spin.

Male and female chakra points spin in opposite directions. They take in and disrupt yin and yang energy throughout the body. Within the body there are seven major chakra points. These allow energy to flow in and around and out of the body accordingly. Let's look at the chakra diagram below…

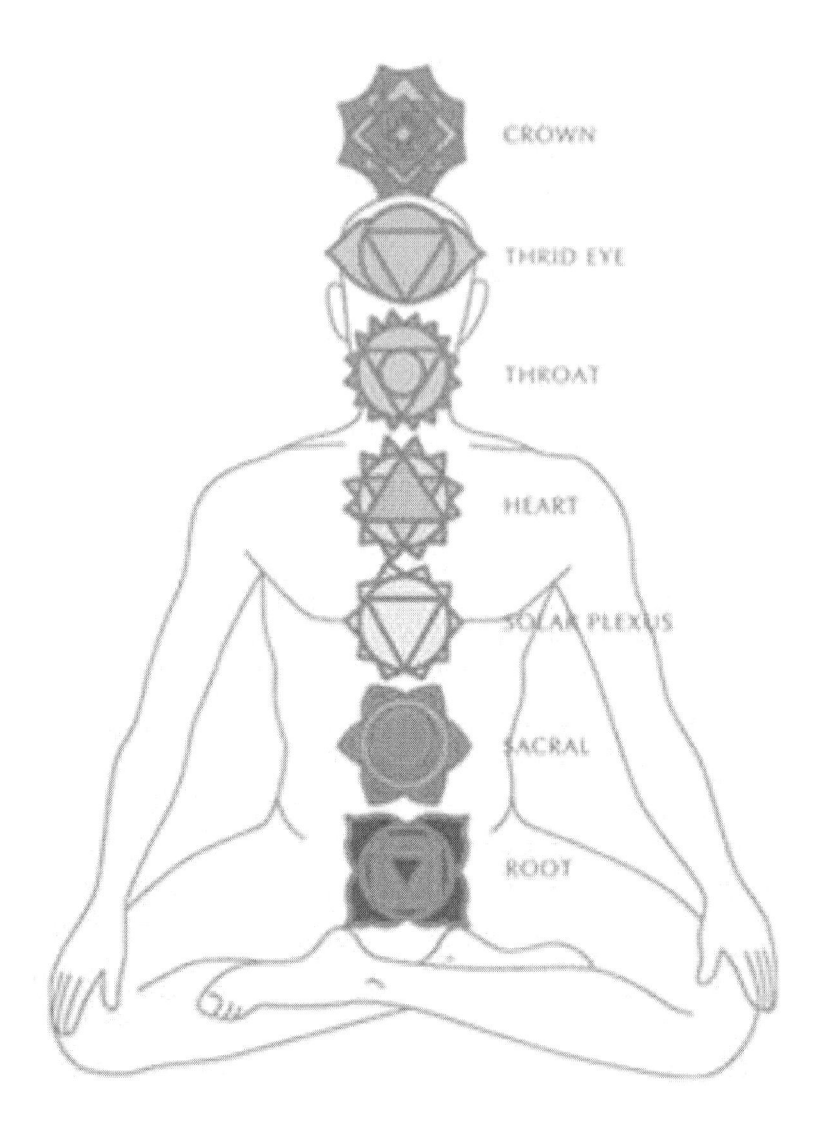

The diagram reveals where each of the seven major chakra points is located. When we work both with psychic and mediumship ability, we are working with the energies of the seven major chakra system. The chakra system is also used within healing. Let's now look a little deeper to understand each one and its meanings.

7th Chakra – Base/Root Chakra – Located at perineum (felt at the base of the spine) also known as the Kundilini or sleeping serpent. Red in colour. Affects the adrenal system, the spine, and the kidneys and represents your individual life force and energy.

6th Chakra – Sacral/ Pelvic Chakra – Located at pelvis area. Orange in colour. Affects the gonads, reproductive system, influences your sexuality, artistry and creativity.

5th Chakra – Solar Plexus chakra – Located within stomach area just below the rib cage. Yellow in colour. Affects the nervous system, emotions, influences your willpower issues, has the power to make you overly submissive or overly dominant.

4th Chakra – Heart Chakra – Located within the heart chest area. Green and pink in colour. Affects heart, lungs, circulation, thymus gland, influences your personal love and unconditional love issues.

3rd Chakra – Throat Chakra – Located within the throat. Light/sky blue in colour. Affects thyroid gland, vocal and bronchial areas, influences your communication issues. Power to speak your truth.

2nd Chakra – Third Eye/ Brow Chakra – Located within the centre of the forehead brow. Purple/ Dark Indigo in colour. Affects pituitary gland, eyes, ears, brain, influences your psychic abilities.

1st Chakra – Crown Chakra – Located at the top of your head. White or Gold in colour. Affects pineal gland, upper brain, influences your connection with your higher spiritual self.

Most of the chakras have a front and rear entrance and exit point. The front opening of the chakra represents your intent to fulfil an action. For example – the front of the throat chakra – a wish to communicate lovingly to others. Whilst the rear end of the throat chakra – exit at the back of the neck, represents your will to do this action, for example – To have the courage to speak openly about your feelings for others.

Often you will find that the front chakra is open and warm, whilst the rear chakra may be closed and cool, through under use.

The crown and base chakra have only one opening/exit, but these may be semi closed or damaged, resulting in low life energy at the base chakra or limited communication with the spirit world at the crown chakra.

Your chakras are normally felt with the minor chakras in the hands. The fingertips and the secondary chakras in the centre of the palms of your hands, as being hot, warm or cold. Sometimes mediums will say they have third eyes within the palms of their hands.

When a chakra is blocked or damaged from emotional, mental or physical distress, sickness can develop over time, in that corresponding part of the body. This is sometimes observed or shown within meditation as a grey area around the chakra.

When someone injures you, whether it is done physically by striking you, emotionally by hurting your feelings or mentally by freighting you, cracks, breaks, shrinkage, or deformity can occur within the chakras. Some of this damage may even be carried over from past life incidents, such as being speared by an enemy through the solar plexus chakra, in battle and result in stomach ulcers in this current life.

Reiki or spiritual healing is very important to have ideally once a month to realign, balance, cleanse and heal the chakra points. Those that have regular healing find they become more aware of each centre point within the body. They also find they can protect it in the correct way to stop energy centres becoming blocked or out of alignment.

Should you feel an energy centre maybe blocked, there are easy ways to unblock the chakra in question. Food is a very powerful way to unblock chakras for instance, if you feel your heart chakra green food such as green apples, grapes, or green vegetables are a great way to open up and unblock the energy within that centre.

The chakra system is easy to understand, the more you can focus on being aware of each energy centre, and you will find it easier to feel healthy in mind, body and spirit. As with the aura there are many books on the chakra system should you wish to go deeper with it and explore it in more depth and detail.

Exercise – The Chakra System

Now we understand how the chakra system works. I want you to sit within the power and feel into each chakra point. Get yourself familiar with how each energy centre feels.

Journal prompt - write down and make notes within your spiritual journal how each point feels good or bad. Get into the habit of doing this regularly as you will find this helps you to understand and identify your own energy.

If you feel any energy centres seem heavy, they may be blocked. Should you feel they are blocked look into the food options for a quick way to unblock the energy around each centre.

Later on, in this book we will work more with the chakras and look at how to open and close them, to allow the spiritual energy to run through our body.

Your Energy Is a Currency. You Can Acquire All Kinds Of Things With It. You Can Lose It. You Can Exchange It. A Question Of Central Importance Is; What Kind Of Value Does Your Energy Create For Other People? – Ayna Leigh Elms

The Psychic Body

Now we have looked at energy we can start to work a little deeper with the power inside of you. This subject is going to be quite long because there are so many pieces to go through and make sense of. I will try and keep this section of the book as easy to understand as possible.

What does it mean to be psychic?

To be psychic means you are more sensitive and open to the energies that are yours, but also the energy of other people and other things around you. If you think of the world around you there are many invisible wavelengths, vibrations or frequencies. When we work in a psychic manner, we can link into these vibrations and they can give and receive information. Think of a radio being tuned in, until it picks up signal it may play a piece of a song then, it might quickly lose signal again. That's very much how it can be when we pick up and work in a psychic way.

Let's say for instance you went to meet a friend and before you met up, that friend had been planning if they wanted to wear their favourite red dress that day. When you meet them, they may have decided to go for a black dress instead, but you may get an overwhelming feeling, and feel like you want to ask them... did you not want to wear the red dress today? Or did you plan to wear a red dress today? Or I see you in a red dress? Your friend would probably answer with something like "yes I was going to, how did you know that? You must be psychic."

What's happened here is the energy they put out about the red dress is in the physical world, because you have thought of them, you have linked into this energy like the radio being tuned in and pulled out that piece of information about the red dress.

This is why I tell people to always be very mindful of what you are saying. Words and thoughts carry power and the universe is always listening. The mind is a bit like a magnet - what we think we become. Wherever possible send out love, happiness and positivity (even if you don't feel that way). You will find you have the power to amplify those feelings back to you.

Intuition is really another form or way of working with psychic energy. How often have you been driving along a road, and you know your turning is coming up, but for some reason you feel you need to take a different road? You're not sure how or why but you have an intense feeling you just need to change direction. Then in return how often have you found out later that day that the road you should have taken ends up being closed, or may have had major roadworks that you avoided etc. This again is linking with the wavelengths around us. We all do this daily, for some the feeling can be more intense than for others.

Are Mediums Psychics?

This is a very important part of development; it is essential that you understand the way you work. It is my belief that everyone can work both with psychic and mediumship energy. However very often you will get people that don't fully know how they work or have not fully evolved and developed their gift. These can be people that are still stuck in some ego or are very impatient to fast track their own development journey.

Quite simply all mediums are psychic BUT not all psychics are mediums. Should you ever go for a reading always make sure you ask what style or way the reader works. A genuine reader will have no issue telling you this. It's important to do this as you may be wanting to link with someone in spirit and if the reader is more of a psychic, they will only be able to offer you guidance.

This is often why readers then get given a bad name. It's not that the reader was bad at all; they are only working in the way they work. But the client or sitter didn't do their research into how they work. It takes a long time to develop and seconds for people to tarnish someone's name, due to lack of fully understanding what they booked in for. I have seen many psychics claim to be able to do both but sadly; the evidence just has not been there. Psychics can give amazing insight and evidence into areas of your life, but the information is coming direct from your own energy. They are not linking or bringing someone through from the spirit world.

On the flip side of that you can get mediums that will also work in a psychic way, as well as spiritually. This means you get the evidence and proof from loved ones in the spirit world. But you also get the psychic guidance side of things as well. These can be just as powerful as sometimes a spirit may not be able to give input around a certain matter. I myself work in this way and incorporate both ways of working, thus giving the client as much information as possible. This in return tends to make the whole reading being more in-depth and more on the money.

What information comes from working with the psychic body?

When we work in a psychic vibration, we are linking with the chakra system and aura field of oneself, but also the person whom we are reading for. Within these energy systems lots of information is stored. Psychics can often link into the past, present, and give guidance or insight of the future.

Be clear to understand guidance for the future is <u>NOT</u> fortune telling. A psychic may be shown insight into a person's future, this may mean the possibility is there. But it's also important to remember that the client will have their own freewill.

An example of this, I was told in the future I would be driving a lot to Gloucester. At the time I had no plans or desire to do this and I was based in Wiltshire. A few years later I was involved with many psychic and spiritual fayres, so I did indeed end up driving to and from Gloucester often. The insight was always there but it happened a lot later down the road, due to my own freewill. Freewill plays a huge part in our everyday lives and therefore the pathway and its future are forever changing and evolving.

How do I work with my psychic body?

What I want you to do is start to look at your own psychic body. This will be something personal to you. Every psychic will work in a slightly different way, but you will find the more you trust you suddenly have a knowing or feeling for something, and when you ask you will discover it is correct or true.

Psychics tend to work a lot with the lower chakra system, from the solar plexus downwards. You may feel you get an overwhelming gut feeling around a person, circumstance, or situation. This is literally the psychic energy being tapped into. I am going to share with you some further terminology that will help you understand the different ways we can give and receive energy. You may find that you are already working with some or all the above ways, don't worry if you are not. As your personal journey of development becomes stronger you may start working in other ways, or change altogether how you work, should you happen be open to this. I started off very much being a tarot reader and did that for two years, but as my development journey evolved direct spirit communication started to happen.

Psychic - The word Psychic comes from the Greek word "Psyche", which means "Breath Of Life", Soul or spirit. Psychics are said to have the ability to see into the human soul and can use this ability to see into a person's past, present, and future. This ability to read the soul is achieved by connecting with the energy field or aura of a person.

Clairvoyants - The word "Clairvoyant" derives from a French term, meaning "clear seeing", and refers to people who can see things clearly in their mind's eye or third eye. Rather than telling the future, a clairvoyant can see what is happening in a person's life in the present, whether that is people, places, or events, and this can often help a person with timely guidance and input on decisions to make.

Spiritual Medium - The word 'medium' refers to the way something is transmitted or transported. Spiritual mediums can transmit and receive information from the spirit world directly but cannot influence spirits; they are only able to pass messages from there. Spiritual mediums are often used by people to send and receive messages to loved ones who have passed over and will usually work with the higher chakra system from the heart upwards.

Psychic Tools…

Psychics tend to work with many different types of tools when offering readings. Some don't use any but depending how powerful they are able to use their skill, quite often a tool can be a handy focus to aid in giving insight. Tools can range from many weird and wonderful things including:

- Tarot / Oracle/ Angel/ Playing Cards - A deck of cards which are used to aid in guidance in a client's reading. They can cover many types of subject matter and help in making vital choices for the present and the future. Tarot tends to follow a set story and structure. Oracle cards tend to be more themed and general and can vastly range in theme and style. Angel cards tend to work with certain types of arc angel energy and can be very free flowing and gentle with a structured meaning. Traditional playing cards often make the psychic work that little bit harder, as they will link in with the numbers as well as what they see or feel intuitively with each card.

- Crystal Ball – The crystal ball has been used as a tool of divination for thousands of years. Early records date back to the time period of the 1st Century AD. It was also extremely popular within the Victorian time period. A crystal ball is usually a clear glass ball. It is sometimes made of quartz crystal of other stones and its size can vary for small to huge. Mystics use the ball to see images, visions and insight within. This tool can also be used in mediumship and physical mediumship, (physical mediumship is physically capturing a change of image or sight with the naked eye) – For instance you might see physical grey or white smoke in or around the edge of the ball.

- Black Scrying Mirror – Scrying, also known by various names such as 'seeing' or 'peeping', is the practice of looking into a black mirror or reflective surface in the hope of detecting significant messages or visions. Scrying dates back to the followings of the old ways and has been used by many mystics, witches, and spiritual people, and is still very popular today.

- Ribbon Reading – Ribbon reading is a very fun way of finding insight and information about a person or situation. This practice involves having a bag or basket full of loads of different coloured ribbons. The client will choose perhaps four or five and the reader will rub the ribbon within their hands and see what they can pick up.

- Colour Reading – This practice can be done in a few ways. The reader would usually have a colour swatch or coloured cards or paper. The client picks out what colours they feel drawn to, the reader is then able to tune into each colour and see how that relates to the sitter. I've seen this done first-hand and it's surprising how a group of people may choose the colour green but, it will have different meanings for each person.

- Flower Reading – Flower reading can be done a few ways and is perfect when you need a quick bit of guidance if you are outside, or within nature. Usually a reader will have dried out or sometimes pressed flowers and then the sitter would pull out the ones they feel guided to. If you happen to be with a reader in a garden or wood, you can pick a flower that you are drawn to and the reader can feel it and see what comes out. (Please be mindful not to physically pick the flower from the plant, as a reader can be gentle - there is no need for a plant to be plucked).

- Water/Sand/Element Reading – This is another older style of reading. You take a bowl of sand or water and see what can be shown and revealed. You may also mix the sand with the water to get more insight into this. Collected rainwater, or sacred water works better and gives more insight then tap water.

- <u>Pendulum Dowsing Reading</u> – Pendulum dowsing is a very popular form of divination. The pendulum can be used in so many ways from healing, to readings, to helping you find lost keys or what foods agree and disagree with you. A pendulum can be bought, or home made. A word of warning with this style of reading - because it is very quick and gives an instant result, some people become very dependent on this tool. I have known of some whom literally live their life around its answers. Please keep an open mind and don't become addicted or solely dependent on this tool.

- <u>Rune Reading</u> – Rune readings have always been a popular way to work. There are two well-known types of runes Norse Viking runes, and witches' runes. Both styles have symbols on each rune. The symbol itself can reveal insight and guidance. Runes themselves can vary in style from crystal, wood, stone, metal, clay and more.

- <u>Hot Wax Reading</u> - Hot wax readings are a very visual way of doing a reading. The client will burn the end of different coloured candles onto a piece of paper, they would then use an iron to burn the wax droplets. This technique creates a visual work of art, the reader can then look into the picture and see what they can see and make out.

- <u>Palmistry Reading</u> – Palmistry, also called "Chiromancy" or "Chirosophy", reading of character and divination of the future by interpretation of lines and undulations on the palm of the hand. The origins of palmistry are uncertain. It may have begun in ancient India and spread from there. This form of divination has always been popular with Romanian gypsy and traveller folk.

- <u>Crystal Reading</u> – This is where the reader works with various types of crystal tumble stones. These will range from all types including rose quartz, amethyst, tiger's eye and more. The client would pull out whatever crystals they feel drawn to and the reader will then read the energies from each crystal that has been selected.

- <u>Numerology Reading</u> – Numerology is the belief of a relationship with a number and one or more coinciding events. It is also the study of the numerical vale of the letters in words, names, and ideas.

- Astrology Reading – Astrology is the belief that the alignment of the stars and planets affects every individual's mood, personality, character traits, and environment. Depending on when a person is born, date of birth, time of birth, and location of birth astrologers can carry out birth chart readings which aid in understanding the reasons things happen within a client's world. They can usually pinpoint huge milestones on a client's journey.

- Tea Leaf Reading – Tea Leaf Reading or to use its traditional name "Tasseography" or "Tasseomancy" or "Tassology", is a divination tool that interprets patterns in tea leaves, coffee grounds, or wine sediments. The terms derive from the French word Tasse (cup), which in turn derives from the Arabic loan-word into French tassa, and the Greek suffixes – Graph (writing) – Logy (study of), and – Mancy (divination). The leaves can reveal insight into a person's past time, present or future depending what the leaves show.

- Psychometry Reading – Psychometry also known as 'Token Object Reading', or 'Psychoscopy', is a form of extrasensory perception characterised by the claimed ability to make relevant associations from an object of unknown history by making physical contact with that object. This style of reading can also be used within mediumship. Say for instance if a client wanted to link with a certain family member, they may bring a piece of jewellery or object of significance to the loved one in spirit.

As you can see from the above, being psychic does not limit the choices of what can be achieved. There is a huge spectrum of weird and wonderful ways you may in time wish to use to work with your own psychic awareness. These are some of the main popular ways in which you can work, and I'm sure even I have overlooked some of the options in this section. (I could write an in-depth book on these subject matters alone!).

Journal prompt - Investigate any of the above that stand out for you. As and when you have some time to dedicate have a go at trying some of the above ways out. Any that you do try, make notes in your spiritual

journal on how you found the experience to be. Don't be downhearted if you find that some of the tools take a while to master. Chances are they may be a bit patchy or 'off' to begin with, but this is the beauty of development. The more time you put in, slowly, but surely the more accurate your insights will become.

What other ways can I build up my psychic awareness?

I want to now show you some easy to follow exercises that can be done on a regular basis to help you make your psychic body stronger.

Exercise 1 – The Psychic Letter

I want you to spend some time thinking of somebody you would like to write a letter to. This can be a friend, family member, work colleague, partner or someone else within your world. Write their name down at the top of a blank piece of paper. Then spend some time just thinking of that person within your mind. See their face and focus on their name. I would then like you to start writing down any words, sentences or paragraphs that come into your mind's eye.

Don't worry about how weird and wonderful they might seem just write them down. You might get random dates shown, or you might get emotions and feelings, you might link with feelings of memory links, favourite colours, and more… as you continue focusing and writing down any insights you should hopefully be able to have at least one page worth of stuff.

Then give this letter to the person you channeled and ask them to give you an insight into how accurate the details are. (Keep this as a fun exercise but be prepared that you may just surprise yourself).

I did this activity once to a group of people I was teaching, and it was fascinating what people managed to pull out. One lady in particular stood out to me, as she was adamant, she wouldn't be able to do it or get anything. She was to think of the lady in front of her and all she could get was a trip to London to see the Phantom of the Opera. It turned out that this lady had booked the tickets to see this show in London the day before my workshop. Whilst this lady didn't write much down, what she did channel was a huge validation to the sitter. This is why it's so important to just give what you get, feel or sense. Don't worry if it doesn't make sense to you, it's not about you as a reader; you are literally just channeling and allowing your psychic body to be your eyes and ears.

Exercise 2 – The Blinded Reading

This next exercise can be done in one of two ways... what I would like you to do is to invite some friends over and work in a small group, (make sure they are all up for this beforehand, as it will make it easier). I would like you to sit in front of your group of friends and ask them to blindfold you. You may use a silk scarf, sleep mask, or towel to wrap around your eyes and head area - make sure you can't see.

Ask each of your friends to sit in another chair opposite you in a random order so you have no idea who is sitting in the chair. What I want you to do is try to link in with this person psychically and find out five things about them, you may also try and link in to see which of your friends is sitting in front of you. Get one member of the group to act as a note taker.

Do this exercise with each member of your group. Then at the end the group can give you feedback on how accurate each of the five points for each person was. You will find by having your vision taken away from you, it will amplify the feeling within your solar plexus chakra (gut area) - the more you work with this gut feeling the stronger your intuition and psychic body will work for you.

The other way you can do this if you haven't got a group of people to work with is find a family member or friend and do this as a one to one experiment. But instead of five things go for ten. This may sound a lot of things to feel into and get but you will be surprised how easy it will become. Get the participant to act as note taker. At the end let them talk to you about each point and its relevance. You will probably surprise yourself with what is revealed.

Journal prompt - make notes in your spiritual journal so you have an account of the exercise. Then if you try the exercise again in the future you can see how your ability has increased.

Exercise 3 – Psychometry Object reading

For this exercise I want you to invite a selection of friends to work in a small group and get each person to bring an object with them. This may be a piece of jewellery that belongs to a loved one in spirit, or an object that holds precious memories of happier times. The object can be as random, weird and wonderful as it can be. What I want you to do is hold each object and see what you can sense, feel, or get from it. You may get images from the past, or you may pick up emotions, you may get names, the possibilities are endless.

Be mindful that with Psychometry you can use it in a psychic way, but also it can be used in a way of mediumship. This means there is the possibility that you may link in with a spirit direct. Should this happen be open to the idea and just go with it. Once you have read an item ask for feedback before you move onto the next item.

Journal prompt - make notes in your spiritual journal of how you found the experience to be. Each item will hold very different energy. So, there may be some you find easier to pick up than others and that's OK.

An extension of this exercise… If you ever visit antique shops, depending how friendly the owner is, often you can pick up lots from items in there. Sometimes the antique dealer may know the history of the item so will be able to verify what you pick up. If you're feeling brave this is another great way to test your psychic ability.

The above exercises are just some fun ways to start working and growing your psychic body. What you will find happens is the more you start to use these techniques; changes will occur within your physical world. When you get a gut feeling around a situation, person, or circumstance you will find it a lot easier to trust your intuition. This in return will help you to avoid unneeded stressful situations, and you will find it easier to deal with life events that come your way.

Once you fully start to master the psychic body we can start to venture and work with the spirit realm.

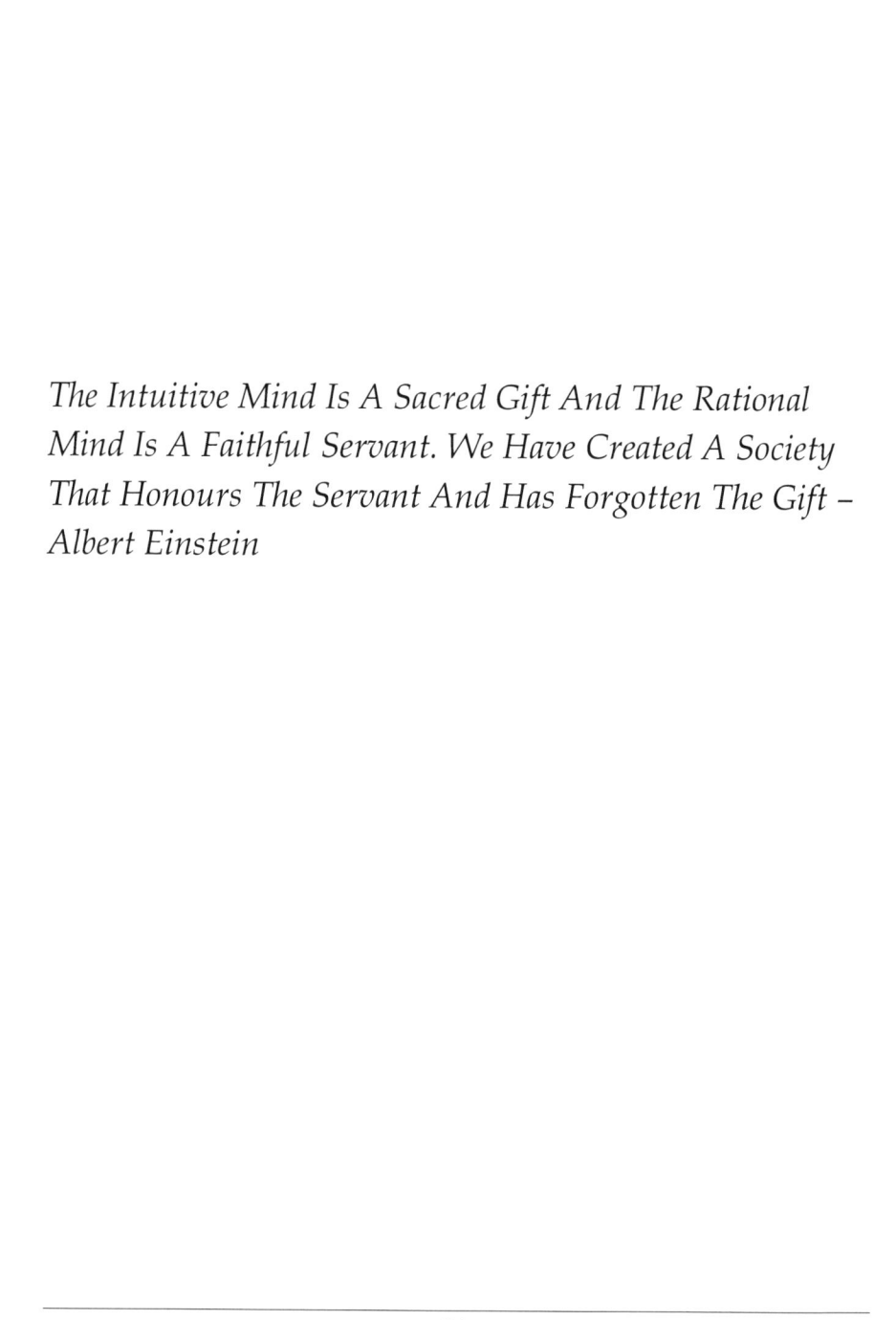

*The Intuitive Mind Is A Sacred Gift And The Rational Mind Is A Faithful Servant. We Have Created A Society That Honours The Servant And Has Forgotten The Gift –
Albert Einstein*

Your Spirit Team

Now we understand the psychic body we can start to look into the power of mediumship. Before you explore mediumship in its truest form, we must make sense, and look at and understand who our own personal spirit team are.

What's a spirit team?

A spirit team is a collection of souls that work with you from the spirit world directly. These will be your spirit guides, angels and helpers but also your door keepers. This collection of people makes up your own personal spirit team. These are people that you yourself may have known when you too were in the spirit world. At some stage your eternal soul would have made the decision to come back to Earth. When that time came to be reborn into this physical reality, you would have come to know or make a connection with the eternal soul – spirit guide that would help you within this lifetime.

As our spirit or soul re-enters this world it forgets everything from times before. But your spirit guide is already there guiding you from the moment you begin life within the womb. This agreement from the higher realms of light is also known as your soul contract. You will have been shown everything you may go through and undertake within this lifetime before you even sign up and enter this world. The lessons you will come to learn the downfalls and the happier times, as we embrace physical life we lose this ability to remember the insight that has previously been shown to us whilst we were in the spirit realm, and so we live the physical journey once more. Being open and aware that our own human freewill can influence the pathway we take.

Another way to think about this… The books I have written in this lifetime, I could go on to read within the next life should I be reincarnated. My spirit would be in a different body, even though I was the original author. A bit mind blowing and overwhelming in a way when you think of it like that. To think a different version of me could be reading a book from a past time version of me, but I'm the same soul/spirit within both bodies. But also amplify and grow in both my character in this lifetime and within the next.

This is why in some circumstances children have previous knowledge of a familiar time and space. I remember once a gentleman I worked with talking to me about this one day. He clearly remembers a day he took his son who was four years old at the time around an old ruined castle. I remember he said how he found it quite scary, that his son was able to give clear insight and evidence into how the original castle would have looked.

He remembered the layers that used to be there before the castle fell to ruin, he also apparently spoke of people and of the wording used in that time period. As well as talking about important dates. This was all researched afterwards and all came back to be true. What my co-worker found stranger is that apparently, they called into this castle on the way back from a day trip somewhere, so it was a completely off the cuff visit that had not been pre-planned. This co-worker was not spiritual at all but even he said he felt it must be connected to a past life or past time as how else would a boy of four years of age know so much insight and accuracy?

What is a spirit guide?

A spirit guide is one main guide that has been ascended to work with you whilst in the physical world from birth to physical death. It's very important to remember we never enter this world alone and we never leave this world alone. Their job will be to protect, give insight, and help you in all areas of your world. What you must remember is they are not here to walk this journey for us, and they cannot and will not interfere with our own freewill. Therefore, if we mess up or make mistakes in life we have to take accountability for that. But by making those mistakes or costly decisions that's how the lessons are learnt, and ultimately how we grow. The spirit guide will try and steer us in a different pathway but depending on how stubborn we are will determine the course of that journey.

For those of us that choose to invest and grow spiritually we can start to work with them. When you make contact with your own spirit guide it can be a powerful and even emotional experience, or realisation they were there all along working with us.

Some people that are not yet spiritually awoken question the existence of spirit guides. What we must remember is within this world there are things we cannot always see but it doesn't mean they aren't real. Let's take a glass window for example… now for those of you who like science glass is neither a liquid – super-cooled or otherwise – nor a solid. It is an amorphous solid – a state somewhere between those two states of matter.

And yet glass's liquid-like properties are not enough to explain the thicker bottomed windows, because glass atoms move too slowly for changes to be visible. To the naked eye a sheet of glass appears to be quite solid and ridged yet it is not. It is constantly moving and changing shape and density all be it at a very, very slow pace. Science confirms this to be true. Yet if I was to present you with a piece of glass window, you would see it as a solid.

Does this mean science is wrong? Or do we just know it works on a different type of vibration energy even though it can't always be seen with the naked eye? It's the same with spirit guides within the spirit world. They are not always visible although if circumstances are right, they can be seen, does that really mean they're not there? You may not see a spirit guide, but you might feel or sense them in another way.

How do I make contact with my spirit guide?

You will have been working with your spirit guide from a very young age - you just may not be fully aware you have been already doing this. When you were a child, did you ever have an imaginary friend? Or did you used to talk a lot to yourself in thought, but feel like you were actually talking to someone inside your head? Perhaps you may have constantly felt like someone was there gently watching out for you? Or you felt like you could see someone out of the corner of your eye? These are some signs that you may have been making contact with your guide from a young age.

You may also have had reoccurring dreams that you were linking with somebody, in times of uncertainty or when you found the demands of the physical world to be too much. Dream time is a very powerful time for the spirit world and physical world to merge, cross over and interlink. Spirit guides tend to become more known to us in times of struggle and uncertainty. It is after all their job to make sure we are safe and protected, so it makes sense when we feel stressed, they draw in a little bit closer.

When I am very stressed one way my guides let me know they are about is by turning off the electrics and or Wi-Fi in the home -this tends to happen a lot when I am planning big events. When this happens literally plugs get turned off or randomly pull out from their sockets in the walls for no rhyme or reason. I now know this is my spirit guides way of saying, stop, disconnect, go for a walk and clear your head. When this happens, I will often go and take my dog Oscar for a walk within the field or woods and touch base with Mother Earth.

To make contact with your guides you have to set up an internal dialog. The best way to do this is via a form of meditation either sitting in the power or you may prefer to use a guided meditation aimed for meeting with your spirit guides.

If you plan to do meditations via sitting in the power keep it simple.

Exercise – <u>Sitting in the power to connect with your own spirit guide meditation</u>

Perhaps have a go at trying a meditation within your mind like this…

Imagine yourself walking along a beautiful pathway within a stunning lush green garden. There are beautiful flowers all around and you just take in the sights, the smells, the colours, the sounds of the birds and insects all around you the peace and vitality that is shown everywhere.

Up ahead you can see that there is a bench, the bench can be made of wood or perhaps stone or metal, however you wish to see and view this within your mind's eye. As you make your way to the bench you gently sit down, and as you do a figure gently walks over and joins you. This will be your spirit guide. I just want you to spend some time connecting with their energy. See if you can see physical features? Are they old or young? The colour of their hair and eyes. Are they able to give you their name? What kind of clothing are they wearing; this may give you insight into what time period they are from.

Are they able to talk to you? If so, ask them questions how they may help you with your spiritual development. Spend time just sitting connecting with them and gather as much information as you can. As they sit next to you just feel at peace and comfortable with their energy, as if we were sitting next to a friend in your physical world. When you feel like you have connected as much as you can for this first time, gently get up from the bench and bid them a gracious farewell, and slowly start to walk back down the track and bring your awareness back into the room.

Journal prompt - Make notes in your spiritual journal on how you found the experience to be. It might be that for the first couple of tries you didn't feel overly too much.

If so, you may have to do this regularly until a connection is built up. If this is the case, I would encourage you to pick a time and day (if you're not able to do this daily). The reason being like when we arrange to meet up with a friend for a coffee or a lunch, it's the same format for our spirit guides; they are after all a friend, mentor and protector you just haven't fully got to know yet. When we set up a time structure, we are instantly showing to the spirit world that we are holding sacred space, and there is a level of commitment and respect there by doing this.

In return your spirit guide will also make that commitment to be there for you, in the same way as if two friends were meeting up to go out for a lunch date. As they do start to link in a stronger way with you, they may start to give personal signs so you will know this means they are around. When I first started linking with my first main guide, I used to get a tight feeling around my throat. My main guide is an older gentleman from the navy called Albert and he wears a tie; I feel the energy of a tie being put on around my neck; this is now a quick sure way I know he is around me.

You may find your guide will work with you in a way of a smell, taste, touch, or other sensation. You will be able to trust that it's them as this sensation will only happen when you are meditating or trying to connect with them. We talked earlier on in the book about trust and trust plays a huge part when trying to work with your guides or undertaking any form of mediumship work. The signs can sometimes be very gentle and only a slight change of energy, but it will be enough to feel it's there.

It's not something you have to do, but if you feel initially you are struggling to feel or trust the energy of your guide stepping in, you could look into the idea of having a spirit guide drawn for you by a spiritual psychic artist. Psychic artists can channel and link in to create a portrait of how your guide may appear.

When my guide Albert first started showing up, I had a portrait done and was surprised how the artist captured him exactly as he had shown himself to me. By having the portrait, you can meditate with this, or set up an altar or space for them to be and it can sometimes help build up a link or awareness with them.

Something to bear in mind, like loved ones within the spiritual world when they show us how they look again it's a shadow of light. They are projecting themselves to look a certain way. This does not always mean they actually look like that, but it's done in a way that you can recognise them. Remember they have no physical form anymore they are a vibration or frequency higher to our own. But within that frequency they will hold the characteristics of the person they show them self as - by having an image of what they look like sometimes it can help to identify changes in energy when the link in.

Something else to be mindful of, like us your spirit guides would have been reincarnated repeatedly. So, whilst they may come through in a certain way, they also have all the energies of previous lifetimes within that one overall state of being. For instance, my main guide Albert would have also been around thousands of years before so he would have been in female bodies, a child's body, other men, possible even animals or other forms of life - so, he holds all those different vibrations and learnings, as well as the overall vibration of being that of Albert.

It's very important to acknowledge your spirit guides but don't allow your ego to run away with you. Lots of people claim to have spirit guides of real status and power, very often you hear people saying they have Merlin as a guide or a wizard type character. Others say they have White Buffalo or other Native American Indians and big chiefs. Whilst they may have these types of character, also what's important to remember is that, that's how they choose to link in with you in a way of identity. The reality is White Buffalo may have also been Merlin in a previous life and loads of other people in between. So, it's not that they are not there but sometimes people create this to be something more than it is. Quite often you may have a normal Joe Bloggs that could also be working with you and has also been these big characters in times before.

In early 2019 I was lucky enough to win a psychic portrait by the very talented Spirit Artist and psychic Anna Trew, www.annatrew.co.uk. Anna channeled a guide for me that was a simple peasant girl. She felt this character to be involved in natural medicine and working with the old ways of witchcraft within healing and herbalism. This was very powerful to me as at the time I was creating my own herbal apothecary.

Spirit guides often link in to help with physical matters we are maybe going through or creating. I have since linked with this newer guide and she helps me in some areas of my witchcraft and healing. To look at she is a very plain Jane kind of character. Nothing extravagant or special in terms of looks or status but very powerful in terms of her way of the world and knowledge for life.

Quite simply if a guide can show how they look to you this is amazing, but don't be downhearted if you never see them, they may work with you in other weird and wonderful ways. I have a guide that I'm told is there, but I personally have not linked or connected with him through visual matter yet.

Something else to be aware of… guides will never tell you how to be or act in a certain way within our everyday world. Very often those that have run with the idea use this as a way to overpower and control others through a situation or circumstance. I have been at psychic fayres before and readers have got nasty or given attitude to the organiser because they may have not liked a spot they have been put in. I've heard some readers say before things like "my guide Cleopatra (let's say) is saying there is not enough sunlight on this side of the room; I must swap with the readers over the far corner of the room". No spirit guide will say this to you; this is just a reader that is consumed in ego being overdramatic and a diva. Stay real, stay grounded, and stay humble.

Exercise – Merging with your spirit guide

Another way we can link and work with our spirit guide is to merge our own energy with theirs. When we start to build a deeper connection with them, this naturally starts to happen.

What I want you to do is stand up and find yourself a quiet space, a room of choice or a place you will not be disturbed. I would like you to close your eyes and take in a few deep breaths and just release any energy not serving a purpose at this time. Feel your body becoming comfortable within the place you are in right now.

Then I would like you to say in thought or out loud that you would like to link and work with your highest spirit guide at this time and ask and invite them to stand behind you. Keep your eyes closed as this will help you to feel the vibrations from them. As you ask them to stand behind you, just see if you can feel a difference in your energy. You may feel slightly hot or cold, you may have a sense or feeling that someone is standing behind you, or you may smell or get some other kind of sensation.

I now want you to ask in thought or out loud for your spirit guide to walk through you from the back to the front. This means they will be standing in front of you after they perform this request. As this happens notice how you feel, you might get a sense of power or surge of electrical current run through you or you may experience something else.

Next, I want you to ask your spirit guide to move their head in very close to your face – so you are almost eyeball to eyeball with them. Spend time feeling this sensation for as long as you feel comfortable to do so. Then ask them to blow in your face. (Don't freak out if you feel a breath or coldness of air, they are just honouring your request). Thank them for this then ask them to move back slightly.

Then, ask them to walk back through you this time front to back. Again, notice how the difference in energy makes you feel – some of the actions you may feel more than others, some you may not feel at all.

Ask them to walk through you sideways from your left side, through and into the right. Then back through the right into the left.

Finally ask them to blend and merge with you as a whole unit, mind body, and spirit. This is where they will step into your physical space and both souls and spirits will connect. You may feel overwhelmed with emotions of unconditional love, or you may feel a power vibration of strength and protection. When you feel happy with this, gently ask them to step back and thank them for allowing you to work with them. Then bring yourself back into the space of the here and now.

Journal prompt - Make full notes within your spiritual journal on how you found each step of the exercise to be. You may notice a type of pattern has formed, and certain requests felt easier to identify than others. This will be an ongoing exercise for you to do but again, always keep notes in your journal.

You may see you always get a certain feeling and in time that might be all your guide shows you, however, that is enough to know it is them. Be gentle on yourself when working on establishing a link with your guides for some it may be a quick process, for others it might take longer. It is a very important part of developing your gifts. You must know or be able to feel or sense their energy in order to work in a way of mediumship as in time it will be the spirit guide that helps you walk with the spirit world.

Can I have more than one spirit guide?

You will always have a main guide that works with you. This main guide is the one I spoke about that helps you from the moment you are born until the day you leave this world and transition to the light. But you may have more than one guide. I have six guides at this time that work with me, it's not often they all work together - some are for my spiritual work, some are only for my witchcraft and others pop in and out when they feel the need.

I also have a guide that works with me purely when I do stage or audience style demonstrations of mediumship. Some of them I can see within my mind's eye or through meditation, others I sense or feel in other ways. As with all of us in physical life we are all different flavours and colours of the rainbow and personalities vary accordingly. It's the same within the spirit world depending on what that guide's job is to do you may feel them more intently than others. For instance, when I am working in a public demonstration my guide for that work is there for confidence, strength and protection. My guide for healing is to aid in letting go, honouring the past, and sending in unconditional love so they feel to be a gentler energy. Some of my guides are only with me on a temporary basis they are here to help me in a particular lesson of life or understanding and achievement of task. Once the task is fulfilled that spirit guide will leave my world, not in a way of abandonment but because the fulfilment of what they came in to help me with has been achieved.

I may also in the future go on and turn my hand to new tasks and new guides might be needed or step in as well. Or in equal measure I may have been dealt all the guides I am going to work with within this lifetime. It's important not to overthink it too much but take these blessings for what they are.

Who are my door keepers, angels and helpers?

Door keepers tend to be more of a silent but protective energy. They are basically a higher up version of a spirit guide - almost like your spirit guide's guide. If you were to think of them as being managers your spirit guide would be your line manager, and then your door keeper would be your spirit guide's area manager. It's not often you will link with your door keeper in the way you would with your spirit guide. But you may sometimes see them as an energy ball of light shielding and protecting you. Sometimes people that have an out of body experience or near-death experience may encounter them in some way.

Angels and helpers, these tend to be again different types of beings of light. When we talk about angels these can sometimes be a form of alien, light being, spirit from another time, place or dimension. Should this type of energy come in for you, you will immediately know that it is there you may see a type of character with lizard or reptilian like features. They come with peace and love so don't feel alarmed.

Angels can also sometimes be beautiful spirits that we knew in life, a mum or dad that was robbed of life early or a grandparent, child or even close friend. Often these types of energy are not spirit guides, but they can become a helper or in some cases a guardian angel. If these were family members that since joining the spirit world have stepped into that role you may feel their presence in a powerful and sometimes overwhelming way. You may find pure white little perfect looking feathers on important dates or times when you really need the energy of these souls within the physical world. Should this happen always collect and hold onto these gifts, as they are gifts from the higher realms of love and light.

Can You Have Spirit Guide Animals?

As well as people you can indeed have beautiful animals that go on to become spirit guides. Sometimes there are known as Totem animal guides, or Familiars. These are again protectors and overseers from the spirit realm. In some cases, although not always if you yourself have had beautiful animals within the physical world, they may go on to be a guide in the spirit realm.

Quite often you hear of stories where someone finds random hair of an animal they owned months or years after they have passed away. Or you might find random feathers or types of skin. I remember talking to one shaman a few years ago at a psychic fayre. He said he had a snake as a spirit guide and one day he threw back the covers within his bed and saw part of a shed snakeskin. He had never had a snake himself and he had never been around anyone with one, he meditated with this snakeskin and this beautiful creature revealed itself to him. He said he never felt scared but took comfort and peace from the experience.

Should an animal wish to work or link in with you again use the above exercises to help link with them. In some cases, you may find an animal links in with you first. This is why it's so important to be as open minded as possible when working with your unique spirit team, as it will be just that a unique set of guides which will aid you in spiritual growth and development with all you turn your hand to.

Who You Are Is A Result Of Choices Your Soul Made Before Coming Into This World. You Wouldn't choose Flip Flops And A T-Shirt To Climb Everest, And You Wouldn't Wear Mountain Climbing Gear for a Trip to the Beach. In The Same Way, Your Soul Chose An Appropriate Personality For The Voyage It Planned – Ainslie Macleod

The Power Of The Spiritual Medium

Before we truly embrace mediumship, it's important to cover off some sections in the build up to it. First of all, mediumship is an amazing gift when you truly hone in and tap into this ancient power. What I want to make clear is mediumship will never bring a physical person back to you in their fullest form. Unfortunately, that physical person is gone forever but through mediumship you can link and reconnect and make contact with the eternal soul or spirit of the loved ones you hold dear to you.

However, when people become aware of what you might be able to do and how you may be able to work with spirit, you will discover that people can sometimes come across quite insensitive or rude, or quite intense and needy.

Fact – All mediums are normal everyday people. They do not have extra special powers like X-Men. They simply work with the ancient powers and energies that have been lost in today's modern world. And like many others within this life sometimes mediums need space to grieve and have their tears, to process the loss of someone close to their own heart centre. A client said to me some years ago now something that always stuck – "It must be amazing to be able to link with spirit, you must be so lucky, and it must make it so much easier dealing with the grief, you have no idea of the pain and suffering you can avoid".

Whilst I know she didn't mean to cause any offence by this I was a little bit annoyed to say the least. As it was only a week after I lost my beautiful uncle. It's very hard when you work as a medium and lose someone close to you, part of you needs space and time to process what has happened. The physical side of you needs time to grieve and heal and take some time out but sadly, the bills still pile up and need to get paid.

No amount of spiritual linking can ever replace the beauty of physical life and having someone within the room with you. Whilst I know this client was unaware it's almost like the grief hit me full on. I actually cancelled the reading and also all booked appointments for a few weeks thereafter. Most people were fine and completely understanding about it, but I had the odd few take the view that as I'm already a medium my own feelings are irrelevant. Needless to say, I did not rebook this type back in, I would have done a disservice and it would not have been fair to put myself through the ignorance of their beliefs or criticism.

There are days when I sit and think about the beautiful souls I have lost who are within the spirit world. I do on occasion sense them; I always talk to them, and sometimes I even see them. I know they are safe in the spirit realm and for that I am truly blessed and eternally grateful. But I would love to physically be able to have an hour of their time, just once more. To have a drink and a chit chat on the sofa, to have a hug and a kiss and to feel their clothes and hold their hands once more.

Sadly, this is part of the cycle of life. But please just know and trust as your own journey of mediumship and development grows don't ever feel guilty for needing some time out for you. You are not an X-Man or performing puppet, you like me are an everyday person just trying to enjoy, embrace and survive the journey of life. Mediums need to be able to grieve and have their space of emotional rest just the same as the clients we read for.

The true job of a spiritual medium…

The true job of a spiritual medium is to pass on EVIDENCE of survival of life of the eternal soul or spirit once it leaves the vessel or body within this physical world. As a medium we are only a voice box for the spirit world, and it is not our job to understand or get caught up within the message itself. Make sure you simply give what you see, sense, hear or feel. Do not get caught up in wanting to know what the message means from your own emotional centre. Too often mediums get caught up in being nosey and wanting to know what the message means - it's not for you to know; as long as it makes sense to the receiver you have done your job.

Please also know as you start exploring your mediumship gifts, you do not have to prove anything to anyone. I talked earlier within the book of how people sometimes change how they are towards you often when we can channel a message it can feel like we want to go and save and heal the world around us. But be mindful not everyone is ready to hear what the spirit world wants to say. Don't ever push yourself onto someone that does not want to receive spirit - we must respect and expect that some people are not ready and may never be ready within this lifetime.

When I was working within the corporate world this was a big area of discretion for me. Looking back, I did overstep the mark and under the circumstances I feel I was extremely lucky. Whilst spirit was really pushing themselves upon me to work with them, it was not the right circumstances to be conducting a reading. I used to really fight with myself when I was chatting to a customer within my corporate world. The grounded side of me knew it was ethically wrong to bring spirit in, despite them literally pushing and shoving me to do so.

But then I remembered back to my days when that first customer walked in and blew me away with the mini reading they gave me, and the weight of the world lifting when my husband Paul knew his Mum was home and safe. That was the trigger that set everything else off within my own spiritual journey. I have talked about that story in-depth within my second book Stranger In This World, in the chapter 'Earth Angel'.

Despite knowing it was wrong I took the view that I may never see this customer again, so I braved it and risked that they would accept. Luckily most did, I only had one or two customers who did not want to know. I know spirit had my back with this, as they were using it in a way to move me forward, but I do feel looking back as my own journey has evolved that it was quite unprofessional, and it could have easily gone horribly wrong. But that's the great thing with development we live and learn and grow from our past times.

But knowing what I know now, I would say don't become an over eager psychic or medium. There is nothing worse than someone pushing themselves upon you even if their intentions are being done in a way of love, truth and hope. Yes, we work with spirit but as I have previously said we are the voice box, we must take full accountability for what and how we are saying or relaying the information of a message - always be mindful that words carry power.

The last thing I want to talk about within this section of the book is remember you are always a person first, and a medium second. You will be surprised how many people try and take advantage of your gifts. It could be that they want free insight or guidance, or they may view you in a way of being like a guru or ascended master and transfer too much of their own energy onto you. Remember regardless of whoever you read for in the future, it is not your job to walk for this person or people.

Always remember to honour yourself and your spirit team first. In the past I have had people really abuse the position of what they are wanting to know. I went through a stage of having a lady messaging me every day wanting insight. It was getting beyond unhealthy and complete energy abuse. I had to make it crystal clear to her I would not read for her anymore and cut off all contact.

Sadly, with this line of work people can become so desperate and dependent it almost becomes like a form of drug to them. Remember you are not duty bound to read for anyone if you feel the circumstances are not correct. Always have firm boundaries in place. It may all start out sweet and lovely, but the amount of people that abuse is really scary. Knowledge is always power so use the insight here accordingly to safeguard yourself at all times.

The Best Teachers Are Those Who Show You Where To Look, But Don't Tell You What To See – Alexandra K. Trenfor

Understanding The Clairs

Now is time to start to develop an understanding of how the spiritual world wants to work with you directly. When we work with the spirit world it's very much like taking on or learning a whole new language. Some key points to be mindful of is spirit are an intense language of its own, like when you learn French or German at school you start off with the basic levels… 'Bonjour' or 'Guten Tag', and then you progress up.

As your vocabulary improves the quality of the conversation increases, in a classroom some pupils master the languages quicker than others. Don't get caught up in timescales or putting unneeded pressure upon yourself, as this will just cause blocks and limitations, instead just be gently guided by spirit as the teacher. This format of foreign language is the same when we undertake a conversation within mediumship. The other thing to be mindful of is it will be processed in a unique and personal way between you as the student, and spirit as the teacher. This is the trickier or complicated part, trying to identify and make sense of how spirit is currently working with you. Also remember that as your awareness increases the ways they work with you <u>WILL CHANGE</u>.

I always remember a lady that sat in one of my development circles for several months. She used to see physical spirit around a person, and she would then give insight on how they looked etc. but she always ended up losing the quality of her messages. She was so adamant that she worked in a clairvoyant manner and seemed quite fixated upon that, she blocked spirit being able to work with her in any other way. I used to say to her on numerous occasions what about trying this or that and being open to the next vibration from spirit. In her eyes she already saw herself as something more than she was - the old subject of ego coming back in.

Sadly, she denied herself the opportunity of becoming a great medium, which she could have been, but she will only ever be an OK or average medium, because she is not prepared to step any further out of her comfort zone. Always work in the way spirit wants to present for you, and a word of caution, don't get too comfortable with a particular format. When you do spirit recognise this and pull the rug from underneath you and work in a new way, often making it feel like you have lost your powers with them and have to start right back at square one. The truth is you haven't lost your ability with them, they are taking your vibration up to the next level, but it can feel confusing and very uncomfortable, as the safety net you had built up is stripped away.

Like the pupil in my circle, when I first started out, I always saw spirit but as soon as I stepped up and started walking with them, they changed the format so the seeing became a lot less than it was before. They made it so intense in the beginning because they wanted me to work with them - once they had what they wanted the real work could begin.

What we need to be more mindful of is, rather than spirit talking to us in voice they will work in many weird and wonderful ways. What we need to do is understand the vibrations, frequencies and waves that spirit use to communicate with us.

You may have already heard or know about the power of the 'Clairs'?

There are eight Clairs which represent the different vibrations, frequencies and formats that spirit use to work within a way of mediumship. You are perhaps working with one or two, or even all of these. What we need to do is become familiar with what each one is, and how we can detect if spirit is linking in this way. Let's now take a deeper look at the Clairs themselves.

CLAIRAUDIENCE

Clairaudience is the ability to hear words, phrases, sounds and more from spirit, some points to be aware of should you be linking in this way...

- You may have felt you heard your name being called out loud, or gentle whispers in your ear. No one is about but you know you have heard voices as they sound so real and true.
- You are very sensitive to noise and sound; you need to have your quiet time within a day and may choose to avoid loud or overcrowded places.
- You talk to yourself a lot within your thoughts and even out loud - you are probably already talking to spirit without being fully aware of this.
- You're one of life's creatives and have a need to express yourself.
- You love to listen to music, a whole range of genres - it's important that you have time to listen to your own style as and when possible.
- You find you hear very random high-pitched noises - these may sound like a popping, buzzing or humming vibration within the inner ear.
- You have always openly talked to spirit even as a child and may have had an imaginary friend.
- You are an old soul on young shoulders. Wise beyond your years, often you're the listening ear for others, and seem to find just the right words to make others feel happy and better than when you found them.
- You have a deep connection with the animal kingdom - sometimes it feels like you understand their thoughts and feelings, and you almost feel you're having a telepathic conversation with them.
- You also get signs or hidden answers through music - you may also find that music comes on randomly whilst driving, or a particular song keeps playing around you wherever you go.

CLAIRSENTIENT

Clairsentient is the ability to get messages by sensations or feelings, using the entire body and complete chakra system to feel and sense energy given by spirit, some points to be aware of should you be linking in this way…

- You can sense energy within a room - positive or negative.
- You struggle to be in a big crowd of people - this could be with friends, family, or out and about in public, busy shopping centres etc.
- You get very strong and emotional gut feelings about people, circumstances and situations.
- You are very highly sensitive to the environment around you.
- You find you get overemotional with movies, music or certain words such as poems.
- You can pick up on a person's spirit or soul's feelings without them even saying anything to you.
- People often judge you and say you're too sensitive and mistake it for a sign of weakness, when it is a sign of power.
- You can physically feel the pain of others around you on an emotional, spiritual and physical level.
- Your moods can change very quickly due to the change in energies around you - for those not fully aware it can come across as a Jekyll and Hyde approach.
- You find it difficult to watch the news and other TV in general.
- You can sense when spirits are around and a change within temperature, both hot and cold.

CLAIRSCENT

Clairscent is the ability to smell fragrances, odours, smells that spirit put forward to identify a character. For instance, you may smell heavy smoke or the smell of whiskey if a spirit likes a drink. Some points to be aware of should you be linking in this way…

- Clear smelling – smelling a scent that does not fit with the environment you are in. This is sensed without the physical nose, but you'd swear that you actually smell the scent or odour.
- Being able to smell random fragrances and immediately feeling transported back into childhood or past times.

- Smelling random fragrances for no rhyme or reason, but nobody else with you can smell it.

(This particular way of working is more basic in some ways but can be more powerful in others. As the smells will be able to really indicate who is linking in from spirit so this way of working offers big validation within a reading format).

CLAIRTANGENCY

Clairtangency is the ability to touch something and receive insight or information. Clear touching – more commonly known as Psychometry. The ability to hold an item or object a ring, pipe, book etc. and read the energy and get information from it and who it belonged to. Please be mindful with this format or method of linking it can be achieved in a way of psychic energy and mediumship energy. Some points to be aware of should you be linking in this way…

- You may go to an old castle or manor home and be transported back in time when you touch the ancient pieces on show.
- You may be at a car boot sale or charity shop and pick something up and get hidden information from the object.
- Objects you touch may feel like they are talking and communicating with you.

CLAIRGUSTANCE

Clairgustance is the ability to taste something without putting anything within your mouth. Often if people have passed in ways of tragedy often with mediumship you may taste blood within your mouth or almost a metal like taste. Some points to be aware of should you be linking in this way…

- You may get an overwhelming taste of something from your past (perhaps not made any more like a type of cake from an older style bakery etc.).

- Spirit may make you taste a favourite food they loved; it could be something you don't like so you know there is no way you would have that taste within your mouth. (For me this would be something like aniseed as I hate it!)

CLAIREMPATHY

Clairempathy is the ability to link into one's emotional feelings - this tends to be used a lot by animal communicators. It can also be used with people that may have autism or physical conditions that affects the way they freely communicate. Some points to be aware of should you be linking in this way…

- You are energy literate and can read the energy vibrations of people, animals and places.
- You feel drawn to healing or empowering the world positively.
- You feel emotions from beyond your senses.
- You likely respond strongly to sacred sites such as Avebury stone circle, Glastonbury Tor, and much more - places that have housed and practised ancient religions, steeped in history, or have practised forms of magick.

CLAIRVOYANCE

Clairvoyance is the ability to see physical spirit, images and clear vision. Both with the third eye, but also with the physical naked eye. Some points to be aware of should you be linking in this way…

- You have vivid dreams.
- You may see a glowing light around a person (seeing a layer of their aura).
- You can visualise and daydream easily.
- You have a vivid imagination.
- You can appreciate beautiful things.
- You may have seen people when you were younger or had imaginary friends as a child.

- You may see flashes or sparks of light, these may be coloured, you may also see signs, symbols or images.

CLAIRCOGNIZANCE

Claircognizane is the ability to have clear knowing. When information comes to mind suddenly without logic, without prior knowing, without reasons or even memory. It is just a certain and strong knowing within the gut, there is no room for doubt; it just is what it is. Some points to be aware of should you be linking in this way…

- You have just known things that turn out to be completely true.
- You have woken up with an insightful answer to a problem.
- You have gut instincts which are always right (like it's become a psychic sat nav).
- You find that your friends and family always use you as an intention detector.
- You have ideas pop into your head out of the blue.
- You always know when someone is lying or being insincere.
- You know what the outcome of a situation will be.

Now we have understood the different ways in which spirit can work with you, what we need to do is try and understand how you yourself are currently working. Identity is very important; the reason why is we need to use this to work out if the information is coming from a spirit source or a way of psychic body. Understanding from the off how you are currently working is very important as this will allow you to avoid any pitfalls within your spiritual work. (It's no good saying you're a medium if your information is coming from a psychic source, or vice versa).

Exercise and Journal Prompt – Brainstorm

What I would like for you to do in your spiritual journal is use a blank page and write your name in the middle of it like you are beginning a brainstorm or spider diagram. Then draw arrows and put one word or a small sentence on all the different ways you already feel you get information from a spiritual place. If you feel that you currently don't get any information spiritually, I want you to go deeper with the energy and see if you can pinpoint anything that may happen in your everyday world, quite often things will be happening but sometimes they are not immediately identified. Understanding how you are currently working will make the language become stronger, and you will then start to form more of a deeper connection with it and start to become more fluent.

Up To Now, Humanity Has Been Deaf To The Universe. Suddenly We Know How To Listen. The Universe Has Spoken And We Have Understood – Professor David Blair

Grounding, Earthing, Opening And Closing Ritual

When we start to work a little bit deeper both with psychic energy and mediumship ability, we must ground, centre and earth our own energy. I cannot stress to you the importance of doing this, it will keep you safe and centred when working with spirit. It will also make sure that only pure spirit with love and light come in and link with you and will help to keep you safe whilst working with the higher energies. View this as an opening ritual which is ultimately what your intentions are when carrying out this technique.

How do I ground or earth my energy?

This following technique of grounding or earthing your own energy is very simple. This should be done before conducting any type of psychic or mediumship work, by doing this actively every time you work spiritually it will become a ritual in itself. The energy from spirit will be able to flow through your entire body thus making the quality of your work stronger and being able to channel more evidence.

To Ground

You can choose to do this standing up or sitting in a chair if you prefer. Simply take in three deep breaths and then realise each breath, you should start to feel your body becoming relaxed. Let go of any stress and strains from the day as you release each breath. With the next breath imagine you are breathing in pure white light, take the breath in deep and allow this white light to travel down through your body, further down through your legs and out through the base or soles of your feet into the earth below you.

Then start to visualise roots, like the roots of an ancient oak tree, emerging from the soles of your feet travelling down deep into the earth. As you start to see and visualise these roots within your mind's eye, you will start to feel like your feet are being planted within the floor below you. You may feel like your feet and the bottom part of your legs are becoming quite solid, almost like the base of tree. You may also feel like your feet have magnets on the bottom and you are almost being magnetically pulled into the floor below you. If you try to move them, you should feel like they are very heavy to lift, and you may feel like it would be a struggle.

This technique is grounding, it's very simple and easy to master; you can also go into the physical earth perhaps a garden or wood, or a field nearby. If you were to go barefoot you would feel similar affects to the technique I have just mentioned.

Earthing as it's known is a very good way to let go and get rid of any unwanted energy, literally with each step you take you can send any unwanted emotions or energies not serving you through the souls of your feet and into the earth. The earth can then take this energy, neutralise it and turn it into something new and positive. The natural elements of the world offer us so much free healing when we become aware of the power Mother Earth truly holds.

When you have grounded it's time to anchor your energy…

Anchoring your energy is actually the most important part within the grounding ritual but it's quite worrying how many people don't seem to do this or in a lot of cases, have just never been taught or shown.

Why is anchoring so important?

If you think of a boat on the water, when it needs to stop or centre itself the people on board the boat release a physical anchor deep into the depths of the ocean. This keeps the boat supported and centred so that it doesn't get lost or caught up, if the waves or currents become too rough or bumpy.

It's exactly the same principle with the roots. The roots are almost the boat going into the waters of energy around them, if we do not anchor them, they are literally floating around within the earth. Now the earth can become quite wet and isn't always solid should the energies a person channels in mediumship or psychic work become too intense, like the boat on the rough water it will just buckle and lose control.

You would then encounter problems with your physical world and would more than likely experience feelings of extreme fatigue, you may feel overemotional, drained of all energy, run down and just not feeling yourself. You may also run the risk of psychic attacks or negative spirits attaching themselves. Basically, the anchor helps to channel the energies you encounter but keeps them separate so the energies don't take physical hold with yourself. It's important when we work with energy to channel it but to not absorb or personally take it on so within the ritual this anchor acts as a firm boundary helping to keep the work you do as safe as it can be. With that theory in mind why would you not spend the additional time doing this correctly?

<u>To Anchor</u>

Continue visualising the beautiful roots and watch these travel down deeper into the earth below your feet. See these roots travelling down deeper still into the earth's crust or core and venturing into the crystal kingdom. Where in the centre you see a beautiful clear quartz crystal point - when you see this crystal, imagine your roots making contact with the crystal directly and visualise them starting to wrap around the crystal.

A bit like the beautiful artwork on the front cover of this book, done by the very talented artist Vicky Baker!

Once the roots are wrapped around the crystal, you then see brilliant white light emitting directly from the crystal. This white light is as a bright as the sun and travels back up through the roots and works its way back up into the soles of your feet. The anchoring part of the ritual is now in place. The crystal acts like the anchor of a boat. Keeping the roots all centred so you don't become lost to the energy waves or currents that you may make a connection with.

When this is in place we can then move onto the final part of the ritual. I spoke earlier on within the book about working a little deeper with the chakra system - by now if you have been doing the earlier techniques I talked about you should be feeling quite comfortable and able to locate with ease each of the seven major chakras on your body. When we work in a way of mediumship or direct spirit contact, we need to open up the chakra system. This may at first sound a little scary or complicated but it's actually very easy and a straightforward process to do.

Please note – when I have been reading for clients, I have noticed that there has become a lot of scaremongering where the chakra system is concerned. I once had a client that was told by a medium they can take years and years to open the chakra centres, and in some cases they may never open. This kind of information is complete garbage and extremely unhelpful. The chakras can easily be opened as they are just another part or extension of you. Like when you open up your eyes, or you open the palms of your hands, the chakras also can be opened in a similar easy way. Please keep this process simple... as it really does not need to be over complicated with false ideas or misguided information.

Opening up the seven major chakras

The white light still vibrating at the base of your feet, I want you to visualise that now travelling up through your legs and into the first chakra, the base, or root chakra located at the base of your spine. You can open this energy point up by imagining a red lotus flower gentle unwrapping its petals and allowing the white light in. Or you may visualise this as a red spinning wheel allowing the white light in, and visualizing the energy turning clockwise to open, or a red fairy door being pushed open exposing the white light, or red curtains gentle being pulled open. However you wish to visualise and see this is a completely personal choice, what's more important is that you feel that energy point on the body and the sensation when it opens - it may be quite subtle and gentle, or you may feel it more directly. This will be a personal experience for you.

Once you have opened this energy centre, I would like you to visualise the beautiful white light travelling on up the body and into the sacral chakra, where you will do the same thing. This time seeing the energy as an orange lotus flower or orange spinning wheel, fairy door or curtains feel the energy of the sacral chakra start to open up.

Then invite and allow this beautiful white light to travel further on up the body into the solar plexus chakra. Yellow in colour as this centre opens and you allow it to be filled with brilliant white light. You should find as each chakra point is opening you start to feel a surge of energy pulsating or flowing through you. You may also experience waves of emotions as certain centre points are opening up.

Next allow this white light energy to travel on up to into the heart chakra - green or pink in colour. As you open up the heart chakra in the same way as the other centre points, just spend some time feeling the abundance of unconditional love purring in and out of your heart centre, and send the love out freely to the spirit world and also the physical world, as it lights up with beautiful white light. The heart chakra is the bridge that connects you to the lower and higher chakra system.

Then allow and see this white light energy travelling on up the body and into the throat chakra, light blue in colour as this centre point opens up. When you open up the throat chakra it may possibly make you feel a bit gulpy as this energy centre opens. Should this happen it is quite normal. Spend some time seeing the beautiful white light within your throat centre.

Invite this white light on up in to the third eye or brow chakra. Indigo in colour as this energy centre opens you should feel a release of power within the centre of your forehead. Spend some time allowing the white light to travel fully into this chakra.

Finally allow this beautiful white light energy to travel on up through your head, and out into the crown chakra. The crown chakra is gold, silver, violet or white in colour. This chakra opens upwards, and as you see it opening at the top of your head, imagine and see beautiful white light shining down over you almost like a spotlight from the higher realms of light.

Once all the chakras are opened you should feel the energy flowing freely from the top of your head, right down through all the chakra energy centres, back into the roots below your feet and into the crystal within the centre. You're connected below as above, above as below. You then visualise this beautiful white light shining out through your body into your aura and creating a beautiful bubble of white light that you are safely cushioned inside of. So only love and light can serve you when working with spirit.

The opening up ritual is complete, before you undertake any form of mediumship reading work, healing or other energy work I would encourage you to say a short opening prayer. This prayer is just as important as the opening up process, you can tailor this to suit your own needs, but you may wish to say something like the following either in thought or out aloud.

Mother Goddess, Great white spirit, creator of all life, I ask for my spirit guides, angels and helpers to draw close and to work with me today. I ask for the highest guide that is able to work with me at this time to draw closer still and stand with me. I ask for them to place me in a golden cloak of protection and place the hood up over my head. To keep me safe and protected at all times whilst working with them and the energies today. I ask to be the highest channel I can be for the spirit world at this time, and that all messages are channeled from the divine light for the highest of good, in love, light and truth. Amen.

You are then ready to undertake and perform any spiritual work.

EVERYTIME I perform a reading whether it's at my home, for a client online, at a psychic fayre, or a public demonstration evening of mediumship, or a form of healing work, I will go through and perform this ritual without question. This style of technique is classed as quite an 'old school' approach to mediumship - in my opinion it's the absolute best way to work. I have tried shorthand versions and other ways, but for me I don't feel comfortable or safe with them at all. Sometimes the oldest and more ancient practices and techniques are the best. I have had in the past fellow mediums and even some students mock me for being so rigid where this subject matter is concerned.

If you share that kind of mindset, I want to explain a few things to you. This style of ritual is exactly the same as putting on a seat belt within a car, before you drive off somewhere or putting on a condom before undertaking the act of any sexual activities. With both these safety precautions in place the risk of something negative happening is greatly reduced. <u>This does not mean that it cannot still happen…</u> You could still be involved in a car accident, or you could still end up catching a sexual disease or falling pregnant, but the risks are greatly reduced.

It's exactly the same by grounding and doing the opening up ritual there is far less chance of you linking in with something negative, sinister or on a lower vibration, or coming into contact with some form of psychic attack. This does not mean that it can 100% stop it, but your options of being safe are much higher around the 95% mark. By not following the techniques I have mentioned within this chapter of the book it's like driving a car with no seat belt or indulging in sexual activities with no contraception - playing Russian roulette with yourself! Why would you put yourself in that position? Keep your work authentic and safe at all times.

I spoke about some fellow mediums and students not following or embracing and understanding the importance of this. I want to share with you an experience I was aware of due to poor preparation and the consequences of what can happen when we allow ego and lack of respect for spirit to get in the way of true spirit work.

I mentioned earlier on about a medium in training - she worked alongside her partner who was also a medium. Between them they had years of experience and knowledge within a circle setting. I think perhaps on some level this in itself was their downfall because they had both been working within a circle for so long that they felt almost that the rules didn't apply to them, and they were somehow superior. A circle is only a safe space to practice, when we work with the general public it's a completely different ball game.

Quite often they would challenge me about my views and ideas, yet they were still paying their money to come into my circle. It is not my job to walk for people, you can show them the way forward but sadly you cannot walk for them. This duo announced that they were putting on a night of mediumship, I questioned them on this and said perhaps would it not be better to be involved in a fledgling night. (Nights where the audience is aware mediums are in training and they have their 'L plates' on).

Their egos where running away with them and they were pushing for a 'one night only with', I wished them both well and hoped it would be a fantastic evening for them. I said I had prior commitments so was unable to attend, the truth was I didn't have anything pre booked, but I had an overwhelming feeling that it wasn't going to go as they wanted. I prayed and hoped I would be wrong - but energy rarely lies.

What we must remember is when we undergo any form of public work, our job is to bring forward evidence and validation, we are in effect ambassadors for the spirit world, so it falls to us to prove there is life after physical death.

When they came to my circle the following week, I asked them how it went, I had already been made aware from several sources that it wasn't a successful night. They began updating me on the fact the night had not gone to plan, the links where broken and they struggled to get any real quality messages to anyone, and it had been a really hard evening to bring forward the evidence. What I found almost laughable was the amount of excuses they were both coming out with. I am not a strict teacher, but I have values and a moral compass, I asked them to talk me through why exactly they felt the night didn't go to plan.

The first excuse to come out was that they felt the audience was not spiritual… first of all it's never a medium's job to prejudge or decide if someone is or isn't spiritual. Quite simply we have no way of knowing what a person's level of awareness or awakened state is and its none of our business to know. When we work with spirit this actually doesn't matter. If spirit wants to link in with a loved one in the audience, they will do so. As a medium if an audience is not engaged it falls to the medium only to get them talking, in order for the messages to flow, that audience has paid their £10 door entry so to dismiss an entire room full of people as not being spiritual is quite frankly a complete joke and very ignorant.

They then said they didn't like the fact that there was originally going to be a break within the evening, so they made the decision to work straight through. Whether you work straight through or take a break makes very little to no impact on how successful a night is in fact!

Finally, I managed to get to the real truth of why the night was unsuccessful… they said when they arrived, they hadn't had time to meditate due to the venue being busy, and so had to go in cold and not warmed up. This area alone <u>WAS</u> the downfall of their evening. When you work as a medium it's extremely important to take accountability for your own actions, whilst the venue may have been busy, I suggested to them, did you not go upstairs into a quiet area or side room? Did you not go and sit in your car? The answer to both was 'no'. Did you ask and invite your spirit team in? - again the answer was 'no'. I was completely shocked and quite disappointed to say the least.

With the amount of knowledge they both proclaimed to have, this was completely unacceptable to be conducting a night in this way. The opening prayer and calling in of your spirit team is so important, the very people that will be channeling and passing on the evidence to you. It would be like asking a band to come and perform a show, but they turn up without the microphones - how would people hear them?

Quite frankly they dropped the ball and they didn't follow or attempt to perform the grounding and opening ritual. How can you work for spirit if you haven't invited and asked your spirit team in to be there? Spirit will never make a show of somebody, but they will use tough love - this was a clear case of tough love. The mediums were so focused on wanting the night to be perfect for them, they completely forget the basic rules. I feel they wanted their name in lights and if that's the case allow the evidence to light the way forward.

The simple lesson from all this was they ended up with big egg on their face because they tried to cut corners. They thought it would work just as well without following the basic grounding and opening up techniques and were shocked to see it doesn't work that way. I would love to say this was a lesson well learnt - I believe one of the mediums learnt from it but the other not so much and wanted to continue to find outside influences to blame - other than the fact they dropped the ball big time before they had even begun.

It wasn't long after that I made the decision to step away from them. I questioned for a time my own teachings, even though I knew they had all the facts and information of learnings, not just from me but from various other places and past circles. I decided to ask them to leave my circle as their energy wasn't right for my group. I wished them well in all they turned their hand to and hoped they learnt from this costly mistake for its was a huge mistake on their part. They lost a lot of respect as mediums and from audience members that night. The moral of this tale is always work from true spirit source, and don't try and blag your way through with your own ego for spirit will always catch you out if you are not working ethically or correctly.

When I teach people development and progression within mediumship, I am very strict on this particular area in this sense of making sure it is embedded correctly. Not because I want to push my ideas on to people, but because this is an area of development that is so important to get right. It carves the footprints on what you will be able to achieve within mediumship, when you have this simple technique in place.

Closing down ritual

Once you have finished all your spirit work it's just as important to close down in the correct way. To close down we basically have to reverse the process on the way we opened up. First of all we start off with a closing down prayer something like the following (although you can tailor this accordingly).

Great white spirit, mother goddess, creator of all life, we give thanks for the love and messages we have received in the divine light and truth. I give thanks to my spirit guides, door keepers, angels and helpers for working with me. I ask for any unused energy to be sent out to heal the world. Everything is done in your name of love, light and truth amen.

I would then like you to bring your attention back to the chakra system. This time starting with the crown chakra at the top of your head. I would like you to close this down, so if you imagine a lotus flower just gently start to bring the petals back into bud. If you imagined a spinning wheel of energy just start to rotate that anti clockwise now, if you imagined fairy doors or curtains be opened just gentle start to close those back up now. Once you have done this in its place you see a healing ball of light.

Then bring your attention to the third eye or brow chakra, where once more you do the same thing, close this centre up and in its place start to see a healing ball of light. Next move your awareness down to the throat chakra where again you start to close this centre point up and in its place you see a beautiful healing ball of light. Then move your awareness down to the heart chakra, still sending out the love freely to the spirit world and the physical world, and also being open to receive this unconditional love back into your own heart centre.

Close the heart centre up and in its place you see a beautiful ball of light. Then I would like you to move your energy down to your solar plexus chakra. Start to close this centre point up and in its place you see another healing ball of light. Then go on down to the sacral chakra close this energy point up, and in its place you see another healing ball of light. Moving on down and coming around to the base of your spine, to the base or root chakra now. Close this energy centre and in its place see another healing ball of light.

I would then like you to travel back down through your legs, back down through the soles of your feet, back into the roots and down, back into the crystal kingdom where in the centre you are still connected to the beautiful clear quartz crystal point. Gently start to retract your roots from the crystal, and then visualise these roots emerging back up through the earth, and back into the soles of your feet, where you see a final healing ball of light.

If you were to psychically see your body, you would see that all the chakra points are now closed, and in their place beautiful healing balls of light. These balls of light start to vibrate and become stronger, until they flood your whole body with brilliant white light. This white light gently emits out through your skin into your aura field keeping you completely safe until you are ready to undertake any spiritual work again.

This is then the closing down ritual in place and complete.

A word of caution…

Always be sure to close down when you have finished undertaking any form of spiritual work. Very often people become lapse or complacent where closing or shutting down is concerned. It's just as important as the opening up ritual.

What can happen if I don't shut down correctly?

Most of us at some stage in our day come into contact with various people. These people may be extremely happy or sad. Say for instance if you went food shopping, very often supermarkets are full of all different types of characters and energy. If your chakras are all opened up in the way of undertaking spiritual work, you run the risk of energy attachments and blockages taking place. We can unintentionally take on or absorb the energy around us which could then lead to burn out, and feeling drained of all energy, or you could encounter more extreme problems such as psychic attack or negative spirit attachments.

If we think of the seat belt idea, it's like unbuckling before your journey has ended. Or to use the condom idea, like pulling that off before you are about to ejaculate - so you then still run the high risks we previously talked about.

Keep your spiritual work safe. In time the more you open and close it will almost feel like a light switch going on and off, but every time you plan to work make sure the switch is on correctly, and every time you have finished make sure its closed and turned off correctly.

Once you have this ritual in place you cannot go wrong.

Exercise – Opening and Closing

What I now want you to do is practice the opening and closing technique.

Just so you can feel the power of the energy within the chakras. Start including this when you meditate, and you will find your meditations become deeper.

Journal prompt - make notes in your spiritual journal on how you found the experience to be.

If at any time you feel like you have undertaken or got trapped energy within your chakra system, there is an easy technique to find and remove…

Exercise – Mini Chakra Cleansing Method

Imagine seven glass balls within your mind's eye stacked on top of one another in the colours of the rainbow. The order of the balls from bottom to top is red, orange, yellow, green, light blue, dark blue and purple. Visualise this stack of balls inside the centre of your body, now imagine a beam of white light going through the centre of the stack of balls and see the white light cleansing each ball. Mentally inspect the red ball and see it glowing with white light. See the red ball as perfectly cleansed. Do the same inspections with each ball in the stack, one by one. Make sure the balls are all the same size. If one ball is much larger or smaller, mentally change the size until they all match. This leaves them clean and cleansed.

*Maybe You Are Searching Among The Branches, For
What Only Appears In The Roots – Omved*

Structure Of A Message From Spirit

Now you have learnt and understood how to open and close the chakra system and put your ritual in place, we can start to work with spirit directly. This following section of the book will look at how we can start to give a structured spirit message.

People often seem quite inspired at the way I can channel a message from spirit with a lot of detail. What you must remember is that has not just happened overnight, that's taken a lot of years of development to get it to flow in that manner. This is a common theme of problem or complication when people first start to develop their gifts they want it to just roll off the tongue, the truth is though that takes time to master and build. This is why having a structure in place is really important and, as time goes on you will be able to channel detailed insight and evidence from the spirit world directly.

One key thing to remember is the word – CERT

C – Communication

E – Evidence

R – Reason

T – Tie it all up

When I first started out learning the language of spirit, I would often dry up and I used to maybe get a couple of random pieces of information that didn't flow, although they would end up making sense to a receiver. Once I was made aware of <u>CERT</u> it allowed me to start to work deeper with my own spirit team. This is then how you start to build up a more detailed insightful message.

The other thing I have noticed is when I am teaching if spirit gives a piece of information and it makes no sense to the receiver, often the student medium becomes terrified to continue the message, because they have been given a 'no' and so they become too scared to challenge that information back and ask for more detail, so they tend to just disregard it and move on.

One key point to remember is that spirit don't just put useless pieces of information into our energy for no reason. Remember with everything you do there is always a reason, also your spirit team wants to work with you never against you, although when we get blocks or panic it can feel like we have become completely abandoned, sometimes we just need to identify what spirit wants to show. I always remember a scenario at a psychic supper I did where this key piece of information is very relatable…

There were six people around a table that I was working with and I was doing a reading for a gentleman and his daughter. I could feel very strongly and matter of fact the energy of his wife, the daughter's Mum in spirit. They straight away started to push for me to get a name, names are perhaps one of my weakest areas. Spirit tends to just not give me their names, not always but in a lot of cases, and so I tend not to ask unless it's actively given - I explained this to them and said should a name be given I'll pass it on.

This beautiful spirit lady went on to show me the Harry Potter tour exhibition in my mind's eye. I passed this onto the Dad and daughter and said, "one of you must be a bit of a Harry Potter fan". They both looked at me quite dismissive and said they had no interest in Harry Potter. "OK, I said let me ask this beautiful spirit to make this a bit clearer". She then showed me the Harry Potter sorting wizard's hat (used to sort out the names) - again this seemed to make no sense to them.

Suddenly with that, the daughter understood the message and said, "Well our surname is Potter and I have a brother called Harry!" Bingo! Suddenly they both seemed impressed with what this beautiful spirit lady had channeled.

What we must remember is spirit don't just work in voice, they work with all the Clair's so an array of ways. Unfortunately, the Dad and his daughter had a naiveté on how true spirits communicate despite me previously making them aware. By not dismissing what this lady in spirit gave me I was able to bring forward good evidence. But I could have quite easily disregarded it as I was becoming a little annoyed and frustrated, that on first glance it was making no sense to them.

Another example of how evidence will always speak for itself… and it will make sense in the end, even if at first it's not clear keep challenging it back and stay in your power. Sometimes spirit will simplify it as was the case here, the wizard sorting hat is all about searching for the correct name. This particular spirit lady was working very symbolically with me.

Within the process of CERT we can also include some key pieces of information that will further help your messages to grow. Know and trust even the best mediums don't always get a full house, and each time you channel a message it will be completely different to that of the last. The same way when you have various conversations with people in your physical world. Some people can be easy to talk to and so the conversations just flow with ease, but others can be more tricky or hard work to talk to - it's exactly the same within the spirit world.

Below are some key pieces of information to aim to channel when giving a mediumship message. Use this as almost a mental tick box or checklist. By asking the spirit that you are linking with this will help the message to have more evidence, and flow with greater ease.

Consider trying to find out and get information on or around the following…

- Description – male or female
- Name
- Age
- Relationship - Who are they to the receiver? (Mum, Dad, friend etc.)
- Condition of passing
- Occupation
- Memories – past and shared memories
- Location (where they lived, or were born, etc.)
- Anniversaries – date and/or month – (birthdays, passings, weddings, etc.)
- Overall Message – conclusion or reason for linking in

The more of these things you can establish the stronger the message will become from spirit. When I conduct teaching within a workshop setting, often at this stage in the programme I get asked the old favourite question, "How do I know this is what is being given?".

We have already covered off and talked in great length about trust. That's the first key ingredient; we have also gone into great detail with the eight Clair's, that's a second ingredient. By now we should have some knowledge and understanding of our spirit team whether we have fully identified who are spirit guides are or not - that's the third ingredient. When we merge all these ingredients together that is how a message from spirit will start to grow and take place.

What we must remember at this stage is spirit will be working in a personal way for you. It might be that already you can clearly identify who is there, but in equal measure you may not be able to. It takes time and practice so the most important thing here is to be gentle on yourself.

Is the information coming from my spirit guide or the loved one in spirit direct?

This is something I am often asked within learning workshops. The truth of this answer is really both… Information is almost like a production line within a factory and it will usually run in a way of the following…

- The loved one in spirit will be passing information *onto*…

- Your spirit team (spirit guides, angels, door keepers etc.) then they will pass this information *onto*...
- You directly as a medium via the senses, thoughts, feelings etc., you then pass this information *onto*...
- The client or receiver of the reading.

In some cases, it can be that spirit will link in with the medium directly, and in these circumstances your spirit guides will oversee the message. I feel (although this is merely a personal way I have chosen to work), that it's not so important to say to the receiver who is giving you the information. When people come for a reading emotions are often raw, overwhelming and people can be in a very delicate space.

What's more important in my opinion is to get the EVIDENCE to the receiver of the reading, very often the client just wants to know that their loved one is safe and OK in the realm of spirit. When we start saying things like "well my spirit guide Cleopatra is telling me X, Y and Z about your loved one", it can sometimes be overwhelming and just too much for a client to deal with or understand.

For me I'm all about keeping my spirit work simple. Often, when clients come for a reading, they don't always fully know how it works, so when we start talking about spirit guides, we could be making a rod for our own back, as they may have no understanding of what this is. The other thing to remember is ultimately the information has still come from their loved one in the first instance, and then onto your spirit team so their loved one is still the original voice box. Where possible I would encourage you to keep your mediumship simple and easy to digest. This does not mean we are lying to a client; it just means we are focusing on the EVIDENCE which is the key thing to prove the existence of life after physical death.

Creating a Spirit Key

What I would like you to do is think about making a spirit key. A spirit key is a personal internal dialog that you will have with your spirit team. The main way to process, create and understand this spirit key is through meditation, either sitting within the power or doing a guided meditation. Basically, a spirit key will give you insightful information when you channel a message - you will be shown something and immediately you will know what it means for you. Building your spirit key is a personal journey between you and your spirit team and this is something sadly I cannot do for you.

Journal Prompt - This is often a frustrating area of development so be sure to have your spirit journal to hand to make full notes after every time you engage and connect with your spirit team.

Let's look at some scenarios…

People quite often ask me "how do I know if a spirit is male or female?" Now, for me when I look at a person and feel spirit drawing close I just know, it goes back to the energy of Claircognizane. So that's how spirit initially makes a connection with me.

What you might like to start doing is asking for your spirit team to give you a clear sign from the spirit key. For example, you may ask them to always stand on your left if they are female and your right if they are male. By doing this request every time you make a connection you should start to feel a sensation. You might get a tingling down one side, or a feeling of heaviness on one shoulder, or a whispering in one ear. It will be something personal, but it will happen every time so eventually you will learn and trust that, that is your sign for identification.

Let's look at some other examples…

For me very often when I ask a spirit how they passed over, I get shown black ink going into water. This took me ages to understand what it meant, at first, I thought maybe this spirit person is an artist, but this is actually my spirit key for cancerous conditions. The colour black in healing work usually indicates some form of blockage or illness within the body. The reason I get shown it in water is often if it spreads quickly as ink in water does just that it spreads and moves about quickly.

As I learnt to trust what this meant, spirit gave me a little bit more and as time went on, they started showing me the Operation board game and they would show me black ink over a certain area. What I came to learn was that they were showing me where the cancer was within the body. It may have been the throat, the stomach, etc. Words of caution when you start to identify pieces of your spirit key keep it personal for you. In the early days when I started doing fledgling demonstrations of mediumship and I very much had my own 'L plates' on, I would say to an audience member that I was seeing black ink going into water.

My mentor pulled me up on this pretty quickly and I'm really glad she did, she reminded me the spirit key is a personal bond between you and your spirit team and the people in the audience do not need to know that is what you are being shown. If the ink is indicating throat cancer, far better to just say "spirit is showing me throat cancer". For in that lays the true EVIDENCE. Once I started to invest more into the quality of the message, the EVIDENCE started to speak for itself - those then became the 'wow' moments within a reading.

How do you know it means illness and not something else?

To use this previous example, I have had in some cases the colour of the ink change. For example, if I was to be shown red ink going into water, for me that is a personal way that I know spirit is showing me a form of AIDS or blood poisoning of some kind. I've also had before the ink being shown as rainbow coloured, when this happens it tends to feel happy and creative, this is the identification for an artist or an arty type person. When I'm shown the red very often it can feel upsetting or nervous even angry energy. Think of the colour red in a traffic light it means stop, but also red indicates the colour of danger. Be mindful that this is my personal way of working with spirit. You may get the same signs, but they could mean something very different.

Water tends to be a way spirit shows me the body - I think the reason for this is because more than 70% of our body is made up of water. The earth is made up of water; it dries up into the atmosphere and condenses back again. Water is a powerful element that holds information, it has memory, and therefore everything that has happened on this planet is stored within water. Every piece of knowledge is in the water - we are made from 70% water and it's constantly flowing through our body; therefore, we hold the knowledge of the world within us. Water can represent emotions... moving, flowing, when we think of a stagnant pool of water that's similar to when we get stuck within the physical world. When we think of a flowing stream this can represent pure and clean energy and being in motion flowing freely.

Hopefully by now you are starting to get an understanding of the importance of finding and identifying with your own spirit key. What you need to start doing is meditation with a clear insight. For instance, perhaps you want to be shown ways spirit link to showcase a passing. You can sit in the power and connect with your guides and spirit team and ask in thought to be shown various causes of death. You should find with each example a unique way spirit work with you will be given.

Often in cases of a heart attack, you may get tightness within your chest or you may be shown the heart area in a black colour, but you could get some other form. Whilst identifying the spirit key, it sounds a little bit scary, but the more you work with the energy the quicker you will start to process and just know that is what it means. The spirit key is something that is forever changing and evolving. As your connection with spirit improves, so the spirit key grows and holds more information and understanding.

The lock and key of a spirit message...

As if this language of spirit wasn't complicated enough! The audience or a sitter if you are working with on a one to one basis also holds a lot of power on how a reading will take place. It's often known as the lock and key of mediumship. Spirit, you as a medium who represents the key, and the receiver of the message is the lock - both are needed in equal amounts. A key is useless without the right lock to open, and the lock can never open without finding the right key.

This is why when you conduct a mediumship message you have to get the audience to speak to you and use their voice, their voice is the vibration that spirit is working with. A few things to remember... sometimes people like to talk but a little bit too much, and they can often come out with lifelong stories. As a medium it's important to put the right working conditions in place, should a sitter start telling you way too much, just simply say "thank you all I need is a yes if it's making sense, a no if it doesn't, or if you are not sure and need to research then a maybe".

In equal measure it's no good doing a reading for someone, and them not speaking to you at all. If they refuse to speak, chances are they are not fully ready to embrace or acknowledge a message from spirit. Don't EVER feel like it needs to become a game of pulling teeth, check out their body language if they have their arms and legs folded, this is often a sign they are closed off. Never feel scared to politely tell a sitter or an audience member off should you do public platform work yourself.

Those that have seen me conduct a demonstration of mediumship; will know that I put clear expectations in place at the start of the night. I will often use the subject matter of the key and the lock as it makes it easier for the audience to understand. The key is the spirit message, but for it to turn within the lock, the locks voice i.e. the receiver needs to give you a form of acknowledgement for the key to be able to turn and open. If the receiver cannot or in some cases refuses to do that the key will become stuck and the information from spirit won't be following freely like it should be.

I also have a 'three strike' rule… this means that after three pieces of clear evidence, if the receiver either cannot make sense, or is choosing not to acknowledge then don't be scared to break the link. It's a waste of time for you and spirit if someone doesn't want to open up their mind. By breaking the link sometimes the receiver may say "actually yes it makes sense", in those cases you can then continue and actually start to work with them.

Sometimes the receiver may huff and puff that you are breaking the link but fails to realise that their own behaviour is blocking the reading from working. Spirit will always try and get a message out to where it's needed, but receivers of information need to work with you, and not against you. To break a link simply take a few sips of water, breathe deep and ask for the next spirit to draw close. Always remember to do this after every reading as the water cleanses and clears the energy of the previous spirit.

Why would a receiver knowingly block a message from spirit?

Sadly, in today's world there is still a lot of stigma and taboo around the ancient practice of mediumship, there can be a whole variety of reasons that someone choices not to want to acknowledge. It could be that actually the reading makes sense, but the receiver was an active nonbeliever and it's left their head scrambled and they just can't understand or process that it's real. It could be someone has linked in that the receiver doesn't want to hear from - a family member that may have let them down or someone that perhaps hurt or abused them. Should you pick up on anything of that nature always ask if they are comfortable for that spirit to link in and work. If they say "no" always respect their wishes and disconnect from the spirit coming forward.

In very rare cases you may have another medium in the audience that doesn't fully work with the ethics that you follow, and they may try to block you. It sounds awful but sadly it has been known and does happen. A key fact of mediumship is there are occasions that messages become blocked or broken. Either deliberately or unintentionally, and all you can do here is try your best, and if you see a pattern you don't like - shut it down.

I recently did a demo of mediumship and brought forward a father figure for a gentleman in the audience. I gave a clear account of how he looked in life, condition of passing, important dates and yet this gentleman struggled to accept this was his Dad coming forward. I then went on to say he knows of a big family celebration shortly coming in. The gentleman in the audience said that, that was completely wrong, yet a friend who was sat with him said "well no, he is right as your daughter is getting married in two weeks' time, and it will be a big family celebration".

Quite simply despite the EVIDENCE being there, this gentleman clearly didn't believe there was an afterlife. He was going through a processing period. By the end of the night despite him seeming quite annoyed and almost angry that I had connected with him he said "thank you" and that it did make sense and he apologised as he knew his behaviour was out of order.

In these situations, it's about remembering to STAY and STAND within your power, this will form a deeper bond with you and your spirit team. At no time did I doubt that his Dad was there for I could feel him so strong and matter of a fact. I also hold onto the power that spirit work with us. There would have been little to no point to make me look foolish in front of the audience. Spirit are not out to hurt or deceive us. With that theory in mind, I knew the block or issue was with the gentleman in the audience. The sad thing was because he chose to be that way, I cut his message short. His Dad may have had more to talk about, but there must be a level of respect from within the audience or it will never work in its truest form. Sadly, this gentleman showed me a lack of respect when it mattered, as well as spirit. I did what I could for him but ultimately he robbed or denied himself of getting a quality message.

The more the audience can understand that you are not actually there to make a person believe, they will usually open up more. In return this makes the power of spirit move in closer and true spirit magick can happen.

<u>**Exercise**</u> – Giving a reading

What I would like you to do is either work with a friend in a one to one style and see what you can channel and pick up for them. Or you may decide to have a handful of friends around and work in more of an audience style way.

Journal prompt - ask for feedback on how accurate the readings were and make full notes within your spiritual journal. Practice makes perfect and quite simply the more you can put into this, the stronger your EVIDENCE will start to become.

Somebody Didn't Wake Up Today, But You Did. That's Enough Reason To Stop Complaining, And That's Enough To Be Thankful For. Never Let Your Troubles Blind You To Your Daily Blessings – Trent Shelton

Psychic vs. Mediumship

By now you should be starting to get a clearer insight into the language of spirit. People often ask me within development "can psychic and mediumship ability work together?" People have different ideas around this subject matter but for me personally yes, I feel they can. This is actually a way I work quite a lot.

Blending the two…

We have spoken a lot in this book about keeping things real. As long as you are aware of how you are working with all the energies then the two formats can blend and work as one. By doing this you can actually add more quality to your messages. Some more strict or structured learnings of development class this as a taboo or a big 'no go' to use the two. For me I think it's about finding the balance and improving the EVIDENCE.

As long as you are able to link in with spirit and work in a way of mediumship and know you are linking with spirit first, I feel it's OK to merge the two together. You can obtain the EVIDENCE from the spirit world, but you can also get the deeper pieces of information from the psychic.

When we work with just the power of mediumship, we are governed only by what spirit gives us so depending on what that spirit wants to talk about will determine how much or how little a subject matter gets covered off. In equal measure if we are working solo with the psychic the chances are you won't be able to give insight into those the client holds dear to them in the spirit world. But you will be able to pick up on things the client is currently going through within their world.

Let's now look at a typical type of a message we may receive from spirit…

I have a lady stepping in close she tells me she is your Mum. Your Mum is telling me that you have lost a wedding ring? I am being shown it's a white gold ring with a very unusually green emerald stone in the centre. I feel it's come off in your garden two days ago, as I can see you in the garden re-potting some plants. Your Mum tells me they are daffodils. Mum says these were also her favourite flower…

As you read the above message you may feel like this is a perfect example of a spirit message. This is actually a message that holds both mediumship but also psychic values. Let's look a little deeper at the structure of this message…

I have a lady stepping in close she tells me she is your Mum – (Mediumship link)

Your Mum is telling me that you have lost a wedding ring? - (Mediumship link)

I am being shown it's a white gold ring with a very unusually green emerald stone in the centre – (Psychic Link)

I feel it's come off in your garden two days ago, as I can see you in the garden re-potting some plants – (Psychic Link)

Your Mum tells me they are daffodils. Mum says these were also her favourite flower… - (Mediumship Link)

As we relook at that message, we have put in all the important pieces. We have connected with spirit directly and brought through a client's Mum, spirit has then made us aware about the loss of a wedding ring. Both those pieces of information have been channeled in a way of mediumship energy. So, we have established matter of fact that spirit communication is taking place, and this is the client's Mum.

We have then dipped into the psychic energy, so this information has been channeled and felt from the client directly, (this part has not come from spirit). The identity of how the ring looked and the fact this client was in the garden two days before re-potting plants. That has all been felt lower down from the gut with the psychic body.

We then have linked back in with the client's mum to identify the flower type and the fact these were Mum's favourite. Once again finishing the message and ending with the mediumship link.

Now had we just linked in with spirit the message would have sounded like the following…

I have a lady stepping in close she tells me she is your Mum. Your Mum is telling me that you have lost a wedding ring. Your Mum makes me feel this may be in a garden and tells me about daffodils. Mum says these were also her favourite flower.

Whilst there is still good evidence there, some of the 'wow' pieces are missing and the message almost seems a bit patchy, and off beat.

Now what happens if that message had just been channeled in a way of psychic energy?

I am being shown you have lost a ring; it's a white gold ring with a very unusually green emerald stone in the centre. I feel it's come off in your garden two days ago, as I can see you in the garden re-potting some plants.

There is still evidence there, but there is no establishing of the fact Mum was about and in spirit, so everything given was more about a current situation or circumstance.

So, on their own merits they are OK separately. But together they amplify and give a lot more power by merging the two messages and ways of working. The receiver of the reading gets a lot more detail and a lot more EVIDENCE. One is not more important than another they are both needed in equal amounts.

When we work with the two energies in this way it's a similar format to signing a song. Some pieces maybe on a high energy (Spirit – Mediumship) other pieces maybe on a low energy (Psychic). It's like the high and low notes needed to sing a song.

Exercise – Song Time

What I want you to do now is look up the lyrics to the following Cher songs…

- You haven't seen the last of me

- I hope you find it

- Believe

You can track these down on YouTube. This might seem really weird at first and you may be wondering what the point of this is, and what has it got to do with spiritual development. As you start looking at the songs you may wish to sing along or just listen to them (this is not some weird ploy to get you to become a Cher follower!). The reason for this activity is to understand the idea of breath work.

When we channel a flowing mediumship message, it can often feel as if we are singing. When we work with the psychic and mediumship energy, like the format of a song we are constantly taking our energy levels up and down - up when we link with mediumship, down when we work with the psychic.

Because Cher has a naturally low deep voice, when you listen to a song by her, particularly a power ballad, you can really hear the difference in moving the energy up and down. Although Believe is a fast song (with some auto tune) you can still hear the changing of energy quickly, so it also works as an example. It's the same when giving a message with the two formats. When we sing a song, we often don't think about the words we just flow with the music. This is also very symbolic of a message, when we just flow with it that's how we bring it all together, and often how the evidence is giving. Very often I am not thinking of what is coming out of my mouth it's just flowing from spirit.

When I'm doing a demonstration, I don't have time to think 'is that coming from my psychic or mediumship energy', I'm aware like a song I'm linking in with both but being very much in control of how that message is flowing. Energetically I know at every point when I'm linking with spirit and when I have linked in psychically. Like when we control our breath within a song. Hopefully by listening to these examples it may help you to further understand and start to strengthen your own messages.

When you practice giving a reading, this will hopefully help you to identify where the information is coming from. There is no right or wrong way here, this is simply a technique to allow you to go deeper with your own gifts. It might be you find you're more psychic or you may feel to be more mediumship based. Finding the identity is important as then you can work with and build upon that.

As I said at the start of this chapter of the book, working with the two energies can be seen by some as a bit taboo. But as long as you can hand on heart know and trust how you're receiving information you can also greatly add value, wisdom and power to a message.

Music Is The Language Of The Spirit. It Opens The Secret Of Life Bringing Peace, Abolishing Strife – Kahlil Gibran

Evidence

Something that I have really encouraged with my own mediumship and that of those I teach is to push hard and find the quality of EVIDENCE within all aspects of your spiritual work and development journey. Quite simply when we ask spirit for help, they will always bring forward the relevant information. When you start working from true spirit source this is something that should be quite easy and accessible. I have seen firsthand some amazing mediums and the quality of what they channel from spirit is remarkable and has left me at times speechless and in complete awe. I have also seen the flip side of this and watched some mediums work that has been of really poor quality.

For me it's important to not judge or criticize the work of others, but I think it's also extremely important to keep things real. If you are proclaiming to be a medium in my opinion there must be a level of EVIDENCE. Some people seem to like the idea or title of being a spiritual medium, but the actual point of the job is to bring forward the EVIDENCE and the VALIDATION to showcase that life lives on within the next realm.

Below are some common pitfalls within mediumship, I am not saying these things to be negative or critical, they are simply some things to be mindful of. Very often those with slightly bigger egos seem to feel they are a cut above the rest. It's so important to allow the quality of the messages to provide the validation for the receiver. If at any time you catch yourself doing any of the following it is OK, being aware of something is step one of correcting the energy. Remember with development there will be times things go slightly wrong or are incorrect, for this is how we learn, and grow, but… you would be surprised how many practicing mediums I have seen fall into these pit holes… and seem to be OK with this as a standard delivery of mediumship… always be honest and real with yourself.

Let's take a look at some examples…

"I can see a cluster of spirits around you" – Just writing this I am cringing slightly, but yes, I have seen firsthand professional spiritual mediums say this to an audience member. (Some mediums may feel this is OK or acceptable) If I was delivering a message like that, I would feel quite embarrassed and ashamed to call myself an ambassador for spirit. Quite simply - where is the evidence? Anyone could call themselves a medium and say something of that nature - with that statement there is no proof of life after death and I think anyone taking that approach is really just kidding themselves.

"This audience is not spiritual" – I have already touched on this earlier on within the book but again the point still stands. I have seen a few nights where mediums have struggled with the energy and rather than taking a little time out to reconnect and focus, they have made a judgement. It is not a medium's job or place to judge or decide how spiritual awoken an audience is. When true spirit communication is taking place, they will give enough information for a receiver to understand.

Sometimes there are nights when it feels hard work - I have had these myself and there was one clear night that stands out for me. But that is about the medium setting clear expectations from the off. If we blame an audience really somewhere en route we have dropped the ball, and we need to look a little deeper and refocus. To disregard a complete audience is quite frankly a disgrace and very ignorant, and completely unspiritual. If you find messages are not following retrace your steps until you find the root problem or blockage.

"You have a Dad in spirit?" – Be careful with this one as it's a common trap that people fall into. This sadly is not a good level of mediumship - all you have done here is ask an open question. It reminds me of my days in the selling world. It would be like asking someone have you been in our shop before, it's an open question so the receiver has to respond with a 'yes' or 'no 'answer. If you feel like you have a Dad linking in from spirit, far better to say something like… "I'm coming to you or I feel I'm with you; I have your Dad stepping forward from spirit". By wording it in a way of fact, you haven't had to get any hints or tips from the receiver, and you are literally telling them who is there and stepping forward. By wording it in a way of fact you once more bring forward the evidence and create the 'wow' factor.

"Can anyone take the name Simon?" – Probably most of the audience can relate or know someone called Simon. Some mediums want to be able to push and give names. This is known as 'fishing', and basically you are throwing a random name out there in the hope that someone responds. There are times when names will be given but again should this happen ask for spirit to work deeper with you. If you feel like you have the name Simon try and establish the link of who he is to the receiver. Far better to say something like, "I'm coming to you I have a guy stepping in giving me the name Simon he feels like a brother to you". Always try and push spirit to give you more. Remember when names are given it's just a way to link, so quite often it isn't always that spirit's name, the name may just be linked in some way. This is why I try not to focus on names too much unless they are freely given.

"Your son will work with you in trance mediumship and always come forward in this way" - Be extremely careful with what you are passing on and how you word a message. The above statement was said to a lady within my circle at a demo night that she went to. I was completely shocked and quite horrified to have found out this had been said. For me this is a big 'no no'. First of all, spirit will never predict something, for that takes away freewill. More importantly what this medium had said in my opinion was ethically wrong. There is absolutely NO guarantee that spirit will be able to link in a way of trance, or with any another medium for that matter.

This is often where mediums leave themselves open to attack. Whilst something like this may have been channeled from the son in spirit. How it should have been worded should have been something like, "your son wants to try and work with you via trance mediumship". To say he will always come forward in this way is setting the receiver and the spirit both up to fail, and any mediums that may be booked with along the way. This medium has absolutely no clairvoyant access to that kind of information so they cannot guarantee that will happen or be the case.

Luckily this lady in my circle came and spoke to me, so I was able to correct some things here. But she could have easily made the decision to book in and see various trance demos. Should the spirit of her son not have come forward she would have felt completely robbed and lied to. Do not predict or give false hope it is unfair, and unacceptable. The son may well try to link but this cannot be guaranteed and gives false hope to a receiver. Do not predict things that you cannot back up, there is zero evidence within this message, and it runs the risk of doing more harm than good.

<u>"Your Mum will die in three months' time"</u> – On the subject of predictions, I have also had on sadly numerous occasions clients coming to me, who have been told statements like the above. Under no circumstances can you either in a psychic or a mediumship manner predict a death. DO NOT GO THERE. It is ethically wrong, and no spirit guide will tell you that information. The clients that I have seen in some cases have become mentally ill because of being told this foolishness. Even if that was to be the case there is no value in a receiver knowing information like that. All it does is create panic and worry. In the case above the client's Mum went on to make a full recovery from cancer and is still alive and well today.

Remember, you are the voice box when working with spirit and always make sure there is a reason and a point when you pass information on. Issues like physical death we do not have clairvoyant insight or access to. Whether you are linking with spirit, using tarot or any other tool do not predict a death, for it only creates worry and stress and will do more harm than good.

These are just some examples of poor standards of mediumship, and you yourself may have witnessed other examples first-hand. Always try to improve on the quality of evidence you are relaying to a receiver and try where possible to deal with and speak in a way of fact… By doing this you strengthen the bond with your spirit team and your own connection will grow deeper and improve.

Always remember the ethics within any reading - to give comfort, hope, support and strength. Often when a client hears from a loved one in spirit it can allow a healing journey to begin, it can be the final closure for a person who is grieving. In many cases it can give somebody renewed focus and give them their life back. Always allow the EVIDENCE to speak for itself.

What Can Be Asserted Without Evidence Can Be Dismissed Without Evidence – Christopher Hitchens

Protection

The subject of protection is perhaps one of the most important topics we must learn and understand. You are maybe questioning with that theory in mind why I have left this topic towards the end of the book? There are two reasons for this really. The first is to prove that protection works with the power of correct intention and to trust the process…

I could have easily put this as the first topic of conversation in this book, but the truth is when we put the correct intentions in place we are protected. I spoke in the start of this book about the need for just two key pieces to be in place when developing your own gifts and self-awareness, unconditional love, and correct intention; as long as you have these two key things in place you cannot and will not go wrong.

I have talked to you within this book about the grounding, anchoring and opening up and closing down rituals. As long as you are doing that every time you undertake any form of energy work, you are protected.

I have talked about the opening and closing prayer, an acknowledgement of love and respect to your spirit team and setting the correct intentions and working conditions. You have been guided and protected already throughout this book, you haven't needed to question or challenge that, you have been able to just surrender and trust the process.

The reason I have done it this way is because, when a person starts to become aware about protection sometimes they over think things, or create a problem that was never really there, and never truly existed. It's important to recognise how and when you need to protect yourself.

As long as you follow the correct principles we have already covered off you will be safe and protected. There may however be times that we need to up the level of protection, or put a little bit more in place than normal…

As you progress and grow with your own development journey, you may find that the energy around you starts to change. Behaviours that you once felt you could deal with or tolerate may really start to grate on you or test your patience. Remember the reason for this… YOUR vibration or frequency level is rising and going higher, whilst others around you are maybe still stuck on the same level and they may continue to stay there, for weeks, months, even years and in some cases throughout their lifetime.

What we must remember is in most cases this type of negative energy or influence is not being sent to cause hurt or harm you. It simply means you're perhaps becoming more empathic and in touch with your true spirit or soul energy. Some people will struggle with this or may be mirroring a lesson that they need to learn but cannot handle or it could be they wish to not see or invest within themselves. This is where we can take control - we cannot change the input of the situation being sent to us from another, but we can change the output and how we choose to respond or react to something.

If you feel like your energy is being drained by what's known as an energy vampire, there are some techniques we can put in place.

What is an energy vampire?

An energy vampire is somebody that is unconsciously using your energy in the way of a battery charger or wanting you to walk the pathway for them. They maybe on the face of things and for the most part are a really lovely person, yet when you're in their presence for too long they are just leaving you feeling tried, low, emotional weak and run down. You just feel completely drained and burnt out when they are near you. A key thing to remember here is if you come into contact with this kind of energy the person is unaware and doesn't realise this is what they are doing, and how they are making you feel.

I always remember from my days within the corporate world, coming into contact with many types of energy vampires. Often when this happens, particularly if it's a frequent pattern, we feel that there is something wrong with ourselves, and run the risk of taking things personally. But know and trust this is just where two frequency levels are not balanced and do not match, they may have outgrown each other and are almost sparking and clashing off each other. I have had it many times where certain work colleagues couldn't wait to start their shift with me. Whilst, I on the other hand was dreading those days where I would have to work with certain staff members.

You can maybe identify with this yourself or it might be you are going through this currently within your own world. It doesn't always take place just within the working world - you are perhaps experiencing this with family, friends, a relationship, clients or even a circumstance around you? It has also been known in extreme cases to take place with animals. This is very common with rescue animals and something I have experienced firsthand with my beautiful rescue dog Oscar.

Whilst I love him and would never be without him and will always continue along the pathway to give him the best quality of life he deserves, in equal measure at times he drains the bones out of me. He has very severe mental health and behavioural issues, through abuse from a past time, so there are times when he feeds off of my energy like a battery charger. He is with me most days and each day presents a different blessing and experience. Some days are perfect, and I welcome those with open arms, but other days can be tricky. For me it's about accepting the rough with the smooth but seeing the overall blessings that he brings, there are times I have had and will continue to put protection in place to safeguard both myself and him.

So, what can be done to help protect and safeguard your energy?

Should you feel like you are around energy vampires in varying degrees, there are a few techniques we can embed and put in to place to keep the unsavoury energies at bay and this will restore some balance and order. So you can be around these people in whatever way you need to be but you're putting a clear boundary and expectation via protection in place. Let's now look at some of the techniques...

- Open Communication – The first technique is if you can, talk and explain how the energy of a person or behaviour is making you feel. It may well be that a person does not want to take accountability or accept responsibility for how they are making you feel, but it's important to give them that opportunity within the first instance. That in itself is a gift and offering of unconditional love. You are not wishing to seek hurts or harm, but sometimes whilst we have become aware of our own energy lines, other people have not. By allowing open communication to take place you may just find that a person surprises you and starts to openly change the behaviour towards you and may even start to invest within their own heart centre therefore ending the energy attack altogether.

- Disconnection – This may sound simple or obvious, but I am a firm believer in the power of thought. For me I very much feel that someone can only seek or cause hurts or harm if we choose to allow that to happen or take place on some level, very often we give away our power freely. Disconnecting from the undesirable energy is so important. You may be asking yourself how I do that. Quite simply DO NOT think about the energy that has upset or offended you. This can be easier said than done, but the more we can shut off and disconnect from it, the more we regain control over a situation or circumstance. Stand in your power. If you are forever talking about how someone has upset or hurt you, you are actually continuously allowing the energy lines to reattach, keeping you in a place of restriction.

To give an example of this: Whilst I have been writing this book, I have had a 'so called' friend completely betray me. Now, I have two options here... I can think and think and think over this situation until my head hurts or I can disconnect and send the energies in question away with love.

I choose the latter. Not to excuse the behaviour of this person, but to free myself from the hurts, drama, and restrictions. By doing this your own personal energy lines stay clean and pure, if I was to constantly be thinking about this, I would be continually inviting it back in. I do not wish for it to rent space within my head. The gift of love is what is missing within this other person's energy field, and so I simply send this away with the power of healing and unconditional love to bring inner peace and balance back into my world.

- <u>The Golden Cloak Of Protection</u> – If you have tried the above options and are not getting the desired outcomes, then sometimes a need for psychic protection has to be put into place. The following technique needs to be done <u>BEFORE</u> you encounter any undesirable or unwanted energy. Simply take a few deep breaths and imagine in your mind's eye a beautiful golden cloak being placed around you. It is perhaps made of a velvet or damask fabric and may seem heavy to the eye. However, when you place this on and around you it's as light as a feather. Imagine the inside lining of the cloak is made of brilliant white light, gently place the hood up over your head. Whilst you wear this cloak of protection, it emits white light as bright as the sun all around you. This keeps you safe and anything negative that you come into contact with is neutralised from negative energy into positive. The cloak also prevents you from personally absorbing the energies that may be around you so you can be within the environment but not be affected or influenced by it. With this technique always wear it before you meet the person or behaviour, and only take it off when you are no longer in its presence. As with all types of protection it's a bit like casting a spell. DO NOT question if it has worked, for you run the risk of blocking its true power. Remember about the power of intention, by following the correct intention in the correct way, when it's placed on it will work for you.

- <u>The Golden Ball</u> – Another popular technique is to work with the golden ball of light. To amply this protection, take in a few deep breaths, and bring your awareness to your heart centre. Imagine a beautiful white healing ball of light, as you see this light within your mind's eye, start to see it filling out from your heart centre.

Becoming bigger and bigger until this ball consumes your complete body and you gently find yourself inside it. You will be quite safe there is nothing to fear, the ball continues to grow and amplify around you. This white light keeps you protected and safe. You can also if you wanted to, imagine the outside of the ball forming a shell, like that of an egg, this again further blocks the unwanted energy that you come into contact with.

- The Snow Globe – There may be times when despite already having a protection in place, perhaps you get an intense flare up from somebody that really tries to invade your personal space, or your sanity and peace of mind. Should this kind of energy make itself known to you there is a need to act quickly. Simply imagine a snow globe within your mind's eye, and visualise it going over the person in question. Seal this with beautiful white light. This tends to immediately stop and calm down the unwanted energy around you.

- Crystals – Another very powerful way you can keep yourself safe and protected is by the power of crystals. I often work with many types of crystal to help with psychic or negative attacks. I also carry a tumble stone crystal with me made of hematite at all times. The following stones are great to work with to help safeguard and protect your energy… hematite, black obsidian, black onyx, black tourmaline, tiger's eye, moldative, clear quartz, smoky quartz. There are many others, but these are just a few popular ones that will provide instant protection. The clear quartz will act as a conductor and amplify the energies of what gets put with it. You may also wish to include a rose quartz to amplify the power of love.

- Amulets – As well as carrying crystals where possible invest in a piece of jewellery that can aid in spiritual and psychic protection. I always wear a piece of clear quartz crystal and a pentagram pendant that has embedded crystals of black onyx. These keep me safe and protected when I wear them. The pentagram itself is very important to me, as this symbol represent the elements of the earth, and is a natural witch's symbol of protection. This is so sacred to me I have gone on to have this tattooed on my wrist to further help and amplify the protective energy.

- <u>The Mirrored Shield</u> – Another quick and easy way to protect yourself if you find the energies around you are making you feel overwhelmed or suffocated is to imagine a roman shield in front of you, within your mind's eye. Imagine the inside of the shield is made of black tourmaline or a protection crystal of choice. Imagine the outside of the shield is made up of mirror, the mirror will send any unwanted energies back to source. This will not hurt or harm another. But it will cut off and block and stop them being able to drain and take your own energy. In the rare case you may be up against a really toxic person or situation, you can add additional shields around you, so you almost build up a cube with you inside. Imagine the shields in front, to the sides, behind you, above your head and below your feet. This will again help to send the energies only back to source with love and light. Please note – some people are wary with using mirrors with protection. But as long as the intention is to only send back to the source you will be quite safe. This will not hurt or harm another. It will not harm the sender it will just re-home where the energy must return.

How and when do I know if I need to 'up' the protection?

If the standard protection needs to be amplified in some way there are usually a few 'tell tale' signs to help prompt and prepare you.

Fatigue – The first symptom is fatigue or overwhelming tiredness. When we undertake any form of energy work we should feel buzzed up, positive and happy. If at any time you feel tired or drained, or burnt out of all energy it is usually suggesting something is wrong or imbalanced. I have done many psychic fayres and private events where I may have read for up to twelve people within a day. Whilst I might feel tired, I also feel buzzed and pumped up. For me if I feel like I need to go to bed as soon as I get home, I know something is off centre or wrong.

Headaches – You may experience headaches after doing readings or a form of energy work. Should you experience anything of this nature, it is again a warning sign that something is off balance. You may get a brief sensation of a physical feeling when delivering a message, but once you close down you should feel like yourself again. If you feel like you have personally absorbed or taken on too much energy something is wrong.

Random Smells - Smelling wet dog or sulphur is perhaps the most important warning sign to be aware of. This can indicate there is a possible negative spirit or attachment of some kind. It can also suggest someone is perhaps causing to seek you hurt or harm in some form. This is ultimately what is known as a psychic attack.

Animal behaviour – If you have beautiful pets particularly dogs or cats pay attention to how they are with you. Very often if we have been subjected to some kind of imbalance in energy, or under a form of negative or psychic attack animals are able to detect this very quickly. Often an animal will start to perform extreme behaviour. It could be biting, scratching, or quite aggressive behaviour. But very unlike the true nature of who they are and their true personality. These are all warning signs that something is wrong and will need to be addressed. I have had in the past people send me hurtful energy in the form of Hex. This caused issues with my own beautiful dog Oscar but once I was able to identify the problem it was then easy to resolve and correct it.

What is a psychic attack?

A psychic attack can only take place and happen when someone is actively choosing to misuse energy. Quite simply it is a form of energy abuse. Psychic attacks are completely different from energy vampires. Whilst energy vampires are unaware how their energy is making another person feel, someone who is causing a psychic attack is going out of their way and choosing to seek and cause a person hurt or harm. For me, someone that abuses their energy within this way is really the lowest of the low. You may be reading this and asking yourself why would someone choose to seek hurt to another? Unfortunately, it happens quite a lot. It really brings into question the status of where a person's own moral compass lies, and how truly spiritual awoken they actually are. But sadly, it's like many things that happen and take place within the physical world. It's no different to when people let others down in some way or physical hurt and abuse another.

What happens if you are subjected to a psychic attack?

The purpose of a psychic attack is ultimately to cause hurts, harm and blockages within your physical and spiritual world. Depending when and how this takes place will determine what might happen. For me I have had somebody psychically attack me on several occasions whilst doing a demonstration of mediumship. Their goal was to try and block me from being able to deliver a night. This behaviour was perhaps due to jealously although I will never fully understand the mentality of this. My guides however stepped in to help block and defend the unwanted energies back, so I was still able to deliver messages.

Had I not been aware of what this audience member was trying to do, there would have been the risk of a complete block and I may not have been able to give or get anything from the spirit world. For me with those scenarios it was after the demonstration that the attack kicked in. My body basically went completely weak and I collapsed, the days after I was bed bound, and it felt like I had gone down with a severe case of the flu. It left me quite ill for around two weeks.

Another time I was violently sick for a couple of days and again my body felt weak and I had the shivers and a high temperature causing my body to go into a brief state of shut down and recovery. With that time period I also had a permanent headache and my third eye chakra basically felt like it had exploded. I had to take a complete break from all types of reading and energy work to rebuild and recharge the third eye chakra.

You are maybe reading this and thinking 'gosh, that sounds quite extreme'. What we must remember with the energy of a psychic attack is that the energy is not natural, and it is extreme. Someone is actively using their own free will and intention to cause hurt and harm, this is often why the body reacts in such an extreme way - it's trying to protect you. Think of it a little bit like when we have a case of food poisoning, the body's natural response is to try and remove the source as quickly as possible. So often we feel and are physically sick, it's the body's way of taking out and clearing the energy that is not serving our highest of good.

What I will say is when you are developing your gifts; it's very unlikely you would encounter this kind of behaviour. Psychic attacks are extreme and usually fuelled by a jealous energy or perhaps hurt or anger. With the attacks I endured, I never personally knew the senders. This is what makes it even sadder and soul destroying, that a person felt so threatened on some level, rather than investing further within themselves, they found it easier to seek hurts and harm on another. Whatever the true reasons for the attacks I will never know. But all I can do and have done is send these energies love and move forward.

How do I clear a psychic attack?

Should you find at any stage you have been subjected to a psychic attack the key thing to do is rest. It's almost like treating the attack as if you had a case of flu. You would need to drink plenty of fluids, water or fresh orange to cleanse and re-hydrate the body. Make sure you don't do any type of energy work until you feel back to full health again.

You can also use the following methods that can help try to rebalance and bring your energies back into self quickly.

- The Healing Wash – Run yourself a nice hot shower or bath. If you are using a bath you may wish to add Epsom salts or Himalayan salt, as salt is very powerful in removing anything negative. If you're in a shower visualise and feel the water running down your body. Imagine the water is made of brilliant white light, and this is cleansing and clearing anything negative from your body. If possible, try and stay within the shower for at least half an hour. If you're using a bath stay in for as long as you feel comfortable, and again visualise the water is made of brilliant white light and it's removing anything toxic. (This method alone will not stop the attack, but it should help the body to repair and heal quickly).

- Meditation To Clear A Psychic Attack – Close your eyes and take in a nice deep breath, do this two more times. Breathing in deep and letting go of anything not serving a purpose at this time. With the next breath take it in deep and just feel your whole body starting to relax. As you start to relax, and your body starts to rest I want you to see coming towards you a beautiful ball of white light. This ball of light travels up above your head and it slowly enters into your head via the crown chakra. As the ball enters it starts to fill your whole body with brilliant white light. Allow it to travel and light up your head, your neck and shoulders, down your arms hands and fingers, into your torso and heart centre, then on down into your stomach, waist, hips legs and feet. Feel this brilliant white light travelling up and down your body clearing any negativity throughout your body any attachments that may be there. Now as you start to breathe out be aware that you are breathing out this brilliant white light. As you breathe this white light out of your body, it now enters your etheric body cleansing and clearing any negative attachments. Sense how this is making you feel as it now starts to travel out to your emotional body, cleansing and clearing as it continues to travel around your emotional body. Next, it moves into your mental body again cleansing and clearing, it then travels further out into your astral body again cleansing and clearing anything not serving you at this time. Now it travels out and into the etheric template body cleansing and clearing, and then on into the celestial body continuing to cleanse clear and release. Finally, it travels out into the casual body. If you were to psychically see your body in your mind's eye you would see brilliant white light inside your physical body and emitting out into each layer within the aura field. Just feel the power of the light cleansing and healing your mind, body and spirit. Do this for as long as you feel is needed. When you feel cleansed and free from any unwanted energy the ball changes colour to a beautiful violet light and gentle protects your whole body and aura keeping you safe once more.

Psychic attacks are sadly something that does happen, so it is important to be aware of this. What I would say is you may be lucky enough to never experience one and I hope that is the case. But should you be subjected to this lower type of energy you now have the tools to heal and recovery from this form of energy abuse.

Negative Spirits And Low Level Energy…

Something that I am often asked as a spiritual medium is how to stop or avoid coming into contact with any negative spirits. Really this subject matter goes back to correct intention. When we work with the correct intention we are asking to only work and link with spirits of love and light. We are raising our vibration upwards to connect to the highest form of spirit world, this is the place where your loved ones will be. Negative spirits are low level energy, so very often they attach to us, it is not that we are seeking them. This is why the opening and closing down of the chakra system is so important, and the protection you put into place. As long as you have done this correctly there is a lot less chance of encountering the unwanted type of spirits. In the time I have been doing my spiritual work I have only encountered nasty or negative spirits perhaps a handful of times. This in itself says to me the correct process of intention works.

However…

If a negative spirit is adamant it wants to link and attach there is still the possibility that this can happen. White sage is perhaps the quickest and easiest of ways to remove any negative or unwanted energy. After I have done any form of healing or reading work in my home. I will always cleanse the space with white sage before I see another client. I will also cleanse myself by waving the sage over my aura and chakra system. This helps to remove anything that could still be about.

The main reason people encounter spirit attachments is when they go prodding something that they may not fully be able to handle. All over the UK and abroad there are many places that are reported as being haunted. When we hear of a haunted location straight away there is a sense of mystery, wonder, fear and the excitement of what the paranormal brings. Whilst this intrigues a lot of people what we have to remember is what it means for something to be haunted. It's a spirit that is either stuck or frustrated in some form, or a spirit that could be quite negative that wishes to not take accountability for actions they made whilst they were alive.

Very often haunted locations are places such as prisons, mental institutions, old castles, pubs etc., all these types of energy would have dealt with low vibrations when in life. If we take the example of prison people were incarcerated for wrong doings, very often those people if they got out would reoffend so they never learnt from the error of their ways in life.

Think of it this way... would you book in to spend the afternoon with someone at a prison that you know has murdered someone, or was a serial murderer? It's very unlikely. So, what's the difference with wanting to connect with a spirit that has murdered someone? Is it just because they are in spirit? As much as your beautiful loved ones in spirit have the same personalities, in equal measure so do the negative spirits. Paranormal nights do have their place, and there are some that are really well run, but having said that there are others that are purely about revenue for the organisers, and when things go wrong the organisers don't always know how to protect from the unwanted energy. If you go to that type of evening you have to be prepared for the likelihood you will encounter a form of negative or nasty spirit.

The whole point of a paranormal investigation is to prove that there are spirits there that haunt a particular space. Often these things seem all well and good until the spirits have become too worked up by people asking to be shown types of phenomena. A glass may smash against a wall, a person may get scratched or touched quite violently etc., this is then how sometimes spirits come in too close into your energy field and attach. I have known on several occasions spirits that have ended up going home with a person that went as a punter to a paranormal night, this is possible although it rarely happens.

Something else to also think about - you usually don't connect with a happy spirit that just wants to have a laugh and joke and a nice cup of tea. Very often people don't know that something is badly run until it is too late. I know that there are some of you reading this book now that will have been to these kinds of events, and others that will go on a regular basis. I am not saying by any means don't go, as it is not my place to tell you how to experience the spirit world in varying forms. But what I am saying is keep it real... If you feel that you want to experience this kind of paranormal work, know how to protect yourself. Invest in you and don't leave it in the hands of the event organisers. Spirit run the show whether we are linking in with the high-level energy or the low-level energy, it's always orchestrated by spirit direct, and in my own opinion it's very foolish and naïve to think otherwise.

Ouija Boards

Perhaps of all the tools within divination the Ouija board is by far the most feared and desired within equal measure. Is it as truly dangerous as people proclaim it to be, or is this all just theatre?

The board itself is just that a board, the danger lies from whoever decides to use it. When you work with a Ouija board its very much like opening up the Yellow Pages. The board gives you very little to no clue if it's a genuine loved one in spirit or a negative spirit playing tricks. I know of some fabulous mediums that use the board on a regular basis, they again make sure the correct intentions and rituals are set in place before activating the board itself, they then close the board down correctly.

The main problem with a Ouija board is sometimes the person or people using it, get bored or are in a rush for something to happen quickly. Very often they will not open up in a prayer or cast a circle of protection beforehand and they will just go straight on to the planchette or glass. This is the first error - there is no protection in place. So, if we think of the seat belt scenario whomever is on the board is not wearing their seat belt. Often if nothing happens people's interest can go quickly and so they don't close it down correctly, this then causes further problems as you run the risk of opening up a portal for anyone to step through. This is often why people encounter paranormal phenomena within their home days, weeks or months afterwards and are unsure of why. They feel because nothing happened on the board itself that particular night it can't be linked with that. Wrong!

When we as people evolve spiritual our inner lights get brighter. The board acts as a portal ultimately for the spirit world but the more people that are working on the board the more light energies are being used. Negative spirits can also be attracted to this light, it can be like a moth to a flame. It has been known for the board to also connect with demon type energy, whether you believe in demons or not isn't really important.

My own feeling on that is often demons are created by our own fears and darkness, so we have almost manifested that on some level, whether knowingly or unknowingly. Negative spirits can also shape shift so the board could be making out that it's your dear old Nan but could actually be something more sinister like Jack the Ripper, the board gives you very little indication on what you are truly working with.

I myself have used a Ouija board a total of three times. The first two times nothing happened, and I am pretty sure my guides where standing in just blocking the energy. The third time was with me and my partner and two other close very trusted friends, one of whom is also a very experienced medium, we had a bit of a private séance. We opened up and started working on the board, for the first twenty to thirty minutes nothing was really happening the energies were just building. We then had a spirit come forward that was seemingly taken on the role of one of my partners family members.

We started asking questions and getting various responses that all seemed to be pretty accurate. We then asked for some slightly deeper questions such as dates of birth, places of birth, important things that were used or done on our hand fasting wedding day. The spirit working the board answered some of them correctly, but some answers were way off, and altogether wrong. We all had a feeling that this was perhaps too good to be true. We asked a few more questions and then decided to close down the session. If anything, the Ouija board left us with more questions than answers. It was about 75% accurate, but for me it felt not altogether true.

When we reopened the board for a second time after having only a five-minute break. We had a completely different type of energy trying to link in with us. The planchette was going crazy on the board and it started spelling out the beginnings of some swear words. It also kept dancing back and forth to 'yes' and 'no' a lot. We knew straightaway this was not a good spirit, as the whole energy of the board had just changed - with that we closed the session down immediately.

For me the Ouija board is a tool of intrigue. But one I feel I don't really need to work with. All the information that came from it, true spirit would have been able to have given me directly, the Ouija board is something I would only work with alongside a few trusted fellow mediums and light workers. It's certainly not something I would publicly do with people I didn't know as you have to be able to trust the group of people you are working with 100% when using the board. The intentions of not just yourself but everyone else need to be genuine and the same.

I can't say that I would never use a Ouija board again, but in equal measure there is no need, want or desire to use or work with one. If you yourself decide to seek out the Ouija board... THINK... carefully before you start using it.

I spoke early about encountering some negative spirits. For me misuse of a Ouija board is probably the one thing that really does piss me off within my line of work. I want to share with you an experience of somebody that came to me for a reading. When I have encountered negative spirits it's never been through my own actions, but it's been having to clear up the mess of what clients have done.

Back in 2017 I had a guy in his early twenties come and see me for a reading. The reading was all going well, the tarot was giving relevant information and I had this gentleman's Granddad linking in passing on things from the spirit world. As I continued the reading the energy suddenly changed. My client was sitting on a chair directly in front of me, I had already picked up that he felt he was in a dark space, but he couldn't really make sense as to why. With that a creature decided to show itself to me, this was a full-on demon type energy, I was being shown what I believe was female although I cannot be 100% sure. Long dreaded type hair, with Maleficent type horns. It literally was like seeing something from a horror film.

With that I asked for my highest guide to come in close and pull us into a bubble of light. I had to act quickly as both myself and the client where suddenly in danger. The reading was no longer a reading; it was about removing a very dark energy attachment that had been linking to this gentleman. I said to him that I was stopping the reading with immediate effect and I needed him to be truthful. Straightaway my guides were showing me a Ouija board that was done and not closed down correctly.

At first the gentleman denied all knowledge of this, I then told him exactly what I had or was seeing. What we must remember is should you come into contact with negative spirits or even demonic energy like spirits on high vibrations they have no physical form. The energy was just that energy but on a lower vibration. It was showing itself a certain way perhaps to scare me, to make me feel threatened, and to try and show it wasn't going away without a fight. I knew I had to detach from how this energy was showing itself to me, and I will admit for the first time ever with my spiritual work I was scared.

Negative spirits often feed on fear. For instance, if you were scared of snakes you may be shown a Medúsa type energy. This isn't always the case but just something to be aware of. Just remember all they are is a shadow of darkness. Stay and stand in your power of light at all times.

The client then revealed to me that he had indeed been part of a Ouija board session that took place within a wood. He had heard of someone that had hung themselves upon a particular tree. But he said after an hour or so nothing happened. Again this was a classic example of foolishness and lack of respect for the board itself. He went on and told me that the board was never closed down and so I feel it opened up a very big portal.

Being in the woods would not have helped, forests and woods hold all types of creatures and animals some that we see and others only some of us may be shown. He also explained this happened around a year and a half before. But he then himself clicked in and saw that's when his own darkness started, this negative spirit attachment was basically feeding off him and making him ill, it had been going on for over that year and a half time period.

Luckily for me I had been speaking to a dear mentor just a few days before about this kind of energy, and how to clear it should I ever come into contact with it. The universe is always listening, and I feel this is probably why that client came to me at that time because spirit knew I had the knowledge and wanted me to use it and for me to be put to the test. I did the relevant cleansing and disconnection work that was needed. This actually took place over a few separate sessions. I removed the spirit energy, but then I did some follow up sessions to be sure all was gone, and normal order was restored. Over the coming months this guy got his glow and light back, he said he felt alive again and didn't ever feel he would get back to that space.

The moral of this tale… if you go prodding a bee's nest, the chances are somewhere along the road if you are not super careful you will get stung.

Don't put yourself into that position within the first place.

As I have already said within this book where there is light, there also lives darkness.

*The Deeper Your Self Love, The Greater Your Protection –
Danielle Laporte*

Ethics of Spiritualism – Code of Conduct

One thing that tends to happen a lot when developing a person's gift, is that they get the abilities, but they don't always know what is and isn't acceptable within psychic and mediumship work. For me with the teachings and learnings of this book, I think it's really important to briefly cover off the ethics, values and code of conduct. Knowledge is power and I think if I was to not include this subject I would be letting you down as a reader.

For some of you reading this book your own development journey is just that, for yourself. But for others reading this book, in time and as your links grow and improve both psychically and spiritually, you may find that you want to work with spirit in a more part time or full time professional manner.

The code of conduct is a preset structure of rules and principles set up by the SNU or Spiritualist National Union. This structure outlines the principles of what is by law acceptable and unacceptable within all areas of psychic and mediumship work.

Very often if you attend an open circle or undertake your own learnings you may have little to no awareness of the existence of the code of conduct. This in my own experience is often when I have seen people come unstuck. They may be very talented in what they are able to do but are at times leaving themselves very open and vulnerable as they are may be going against the major principles of the code of conduct.

By being aware of this structure you can add ethical values into all areas of your spiritual work.

The Code Of Conduct – The Do's

- Do install optimism – Try to see beyond the bad events to better times, of course there may be obstacles ahead but help the client realise the power of positive thinking.

- Do stress freewill – A prediction that inhabits a person's growth is worthless. We all have the power and freedom of freewill and this largely affects what may happen as opposed to what will happen.

- Do give evidence – Try to give qualified facts about the sitter's life or those they hold dear to them in spirit. Do not just talk about a lot of junk from your own ego. Establish facts and evidence about the sitter and their life. For mediumship focus on proof of survival for example – how the person died, their character, attitudes and habits, stories from their life, important dates or things that have been said to prove that true spirit communication is taking place.

- Do cultivate spiritual values – Make your daily life part of your spiritual work. Try to change your attitudes and develop good spiritual habits, this will help you in building your relationships with your spirit guides, angels and helpers. (For example – if you never bother to mediate, don't be surprised if you struggle to link and identify who is working with you).

- Do be good humoured – Try to spread a little happiness and laughter with your spiritual work. The spirit realm is after all a place of eternal love and peace.

- Do improve yourself – Development is a lifelong process, always try to improve upon the quality of your links and evidence from spirit. Also, please keep it real, stay grounded and humble within your sacred heart.

- Do remember – Spirit is communicating and working through you, don't allow the ego to take over. Remember to thank your spirit team for coming to work with you.

- If you choose to read in a professional manner or offer a paid service or do any form of public psychic or mediumship work, by law you must obtain public liability insurance.

- With all types of reading please make it clear that by law this is for entertainment and experiment purposes only. You must be 18+ to have a reading.

- If you decide to work in a spiritual church or centre to do a night of clairvoyance, you will be required to do an opening and closing prayer. Some churches may also expect an address or piece of philosophy.

The Code Of Conduct – The Don'ts

- Don't predict a death – A genuine psychic or medium will know that this is impossible. It is not something that we have clairvoyant access to, and no spirit guide will give you that sort of information. (You may well be shown a scenario but remember the pathway is forever changing and evolving).

- Don't predict accidents or other calamities – This will distress the recipient of your communication. If you see a fall down a step you can say – is there a loose step that may need attention?

- Don't play the doctor – Under no circumstances suggest someone should go against the doctor's advice, diagnose an illness or prescribe medication. You can advise someone goes to see their doctor if you are aware they have some worries. Or if you are know someone is suffering with back pain you can suggest forms of holistic therapies alongside the advice of a doctor, for example a massage or reflexology treatment.

- Don't be the guru – Please stress that you are only an ordinary person, or the sitter may think that you're the only person in the world that can solve their problems. This is energy abuse it is never a reader's job to walk the journey for a client. Remember some clients have no awareness of boundaries. Psychiatrists call this transference.

- Don't make exaggerated claims – You cannot guarantee that you can mediumistically communicate with the loved one in spirit that the client wishes to hear from, so should they come with larger than life expectations make it clear from the off. Otherwise this could be construed as claiming to 'calling up the dead'. Nor can you guarantee to solve their problems. Every sitting is a unique experiment.

- Don't embellish clairvoyance – Keep your evidence clear. If you dry up stop the reading. It's no good adding a load of junk from your own subconscious to the reading. Remember to keep in the flow, once the client recognises who you have linked in with there is no need to keep saying how they look etc., move on to the actual roots of the message.

- Don't force yourself onto people – There is nothing worse than the overeager psychic that pushes clairvoyance onto people. Some people do not want to hear from their Granddad in spirit whilst waiting for a bus. It is not appropriate to go around reading for people when they are not aware of it.

- Don't use tools you are not capable of - like Ouija boards, these should only be used under controlled and supervised circumstances. Most mediums do not like or will not agree to work with Ouija boards. We have already talked in depth about this subject matter and the points still stand.

- Don't claim to be something you are not – Make sure you know how you work before you start putting yourself out there. Psychic, tarot reader, spiritual medium or you may be a mix of all these. Keep all your spiritual work as ethical as possible and make sure your own moral compass is always pointing in the right direction.

- Don't give away your power – Don't ever feel like you need to compete with another. You have your own unique bond with spirit as does any other reader. Do not feel threatened by what somebody else is doing, always hold and stay in your own authentic power.

The above key points should all be pretty self-explanatory, but sadly it is surprising sometimes how people seem to have no awareness for the principles of mediumship. Try and embed the basics from the off and you cannot go wrong.

The final point I wish to add to this list is…

- **Don't forget to write down things that happen within your own spiritual journal – depending how much work you do you may find you have more than one journal and that is OK. But it is a key ingredient that can visually help you move forward. For when you read through it you will be able to see first hand how the quality of work is changing and evolving for the better.**

A Tree That Wants To touch The Sky Must Extend Its Roots Into The Earth. The More It Wants To Rise Upwards, The More It Has To Grow Downwards. So To Rise In Life, We Must Be Down to Earth, Humble And Grateful – Tushar Verma

Staying Authentic

Before this book comes to a close, I wanted to talk to you a little about the power of staying authentic. This is perhaps one of the most important gifts you can truly give yourself. As your journey of self-development evolves people may form ideas and opinions on how you should and shouldn't be working, or what you should and shouldn't be doing. Always be guided by the inner light within your own heart centre.

When I first started out on my road of self-development it was very much the power of the tarot that found me. I spend over two years perfecting and learning the craft of tarot before I deepened my journey of self-development. I had some amazing mentors within my life, but I clearly remember one comment that always stands out by a particular mentor. "You are a good card reader but that is all you are and all you ever will be". I found this comment a little bit hard hitting, to say the least and slightly ignorant, this mentor could see my light but in equal measure felt not worthy of celebrating it, and on some level wanted to pull or hold me back.

Some people have questioned my love for tarot and almost overlooked it as a secondary ability. For me tarot was and always will be my first love, and my true tool of divination.

I want to share with you an experience as to why I feel so connected to the power of tarot. As I have already said I spent the first two years really developing, practicing and perfecting the art of being able to read for people with the tarot. Friends and family knew I was getting good feedback and positive results and so they started to encourage me to start charging for my work. I felt so scared and nervous to charge or put a price onto my spiritual work so I decided at that time this was really nothing more than a hobby and I would charge five pounds for an hour reading.

I put it out there and didn't expect for too much to come back. However, a young lady in her mid-thirties contacted me and wanted to book in. At that time, I was still very much involved with my full time day job, and so trying to find a suitable time and date wasn't always easy - often I would be working a long shift to then turn around and open up my home in the evening to do the odd reading. We arranged to meet on a Friday evening at 8 pm. This beautiful lady turned up, with a big black rucksack on her back and lovely warm smile. I invited her in, and we went into my little spare room that I had set up as I reading space.

I started to conduct the reading and allowed the magick of the tarot to guide me through. We ended up going well over the hour but that was OK, I've always felt that readings will be as long as they need to be. I've since tried to get better with my own time keeping but this is an ongoing area of development for me.

The reading came to an end and we both had gentle tears in our eyes, it was a powerful deep reading, and the cards presented a lot of guidance for the client. She grabbed her black rucksack of the floor and put it onto her lap, she opened it up and went to an inside pocket. She unzipped the pocket and handed me the five pound note and it felt really powerful that somebody valued my work enough to pay me. But then something even more powerful happened, she went deeper into the rucksack and pulled out a load of thick rope with a premade noose on the end. She handed this to me and said thank you so much I will not be needing this now. She then went on to tell me that this year had been so dark for her, and after her reading she was planning to go over to Longleat Forest and hang herself.

She had already picked out where she had planned to do this and had even found what she called the perfect hanging tree.

The hour and a half I had spent with her in my little room being able to offer her the chance to speak, but also to listen for her voice to be truly heard was the starting point of this lady's healing journey. Through the magick of the tarot she could see in black and white that the story she was stuck in didn't need to be this way. All she had to do was take a deep breath and turn the page in her own book of life.

This for me was an experience that I will never forget, that feeling of being able to make somebody feel that little bit better than when they first walked into the room. This is what the true gift is all about. Clients have said to me on and off over the years you have saved me, and I find this sometimes a bit uncomfortable to be truthful but one thing I do know is that on this particular occasion I did save this lady that night through the power of tarot.

So, if you ever find that someone overlooks your worth, or puts you down because they view you as nothing more than just a good card reader. Remember that you do not need to seek their approval, the only person that needs to judge your work is whomever you are reading for.

Sometimes a good card reader is all you need to be, to restore the light and love within another's heart centre.

As my own journey of progression has evolved it hasn't always been easy. Although I have always been a big believer in sometimes the things that challenge us the most, also offer us the best rewards and outcomes.

Being an open male witch at times has often divided opinion. But it's important to remember that witchcraft is something that is unique and personal for me, it's not something that I need to seek approval from another for.

I always remember I was invited to do an evening of mediumship at a small little SNU church within Wiltshire. For me and my own style of working with the spirit world I like to kind of go straight in with the mediumship. Whilst I can do philosophy this isn't something that comes so naturally. For me I much prefer an open prayer and then leave the evening within the hands of spirit.

This particular church made out they were quite free spirited for being SNU. I thought OK nothing to really lose and I felt very blessed that I had been asked to come and serve their church. However, as time went on I was suddenly asked 'could I include a short piece of philosophy and do a talk around this'. I was also asked 'could I not talk too much or at all about my witchcraft and pagan ways'. For what was meant to be a very free spirited evening I was finding there were just too many rules and regulations.

As time went on and the date grew nearer, I actually came down with a really bad bug so had to cancel. I got rebooked and a new date was agreed, yet again as time got closer, I kept falling ill. This happened a total of three times - three is a very powerful number. I decided that clearly this was a space the spirit world didn't want me to be in, and really looking at it now it wouldn't have been the right space. The church was just that a church and they had their own structure of how they wanted the mediumship to be delivered. It wasn't necessarily the way I would or could work.

I made the decision to cancel any forthcoming events and explained my reasons for this. I didn't get nasty or rude I just made it clear that being an open male witch I worked and lived a certain way. The more I thought about this the more I thought, I'm actually not prepared to switch off from being a witch for one night because you want me to present mediumship in the format you would like. For me that is not authentic.

Now don't get me wrong there are many mediums I know that would have very quickly altered and changed their format to comply. For me I feel this was a gift from spirit about boundaries. I was not prepared to change who I was. It reminded me off the pattern all those years ago at school with the bullies wanting me to act upon their desires. What was really interesting was rather than accepting my wishes and parting ways with love and light the organiser got very rude and aggressive saying 'well actually after your recent behaviour we wouldn't want to pre-book you or have any dealings with you'.

Again, this showed to me a classic example of how people can quickly turn on you when you stay in your power. Up until the point that I bowed out graceful the organiser had been nicer than nice with me. But as soon as it was made clear I wasn't going to alter who I was for their needs or desires; they became very rude. I felt the whole experience revealed more about them and less about me.

Perhaps within my own journey of development one thing that I always remember is something I was told by a mentor. I believe in their own way they were trying to care for and protect me. But the following piece of advice was something I personally just could not or would not accept. I was told that I was far too nice, and that I needed to change my behaviour. To survive in this business of spiritualism I would need to grow a very thick skin and toughen up or I would be eaten up and spat back out.

For me all growing up the pattern has been the above statement. But I always feel if you are true to your heart centre and can have the bravery to stand within your own power and light, why would you try and change or deny that. With my own journey of development it hasn't been so much about finding who I truly am, it's been about celebrating who I have always been and the fact I don't give my power away to serve another person. It was never really about finding who I was; the gift was more celebrating and accepting the unique energy of my true spirit.

If I have to change my ways to fit into a world or structure, I would rather not be there in the first place. I have found that by always being the true you is the greatest form of existence we can have whilst we are here within this lifetime. So as much as I love and hold respect for that particular mentor, I cannot and do not agree with their advice on that particular occasion.

The final story I want to share with you in this section of the book is one that makes me laugh and smile. Earlier on in 2019 in the power of the heat wave and summertime, I read for a beautiful lady. She came to me on one of the hottest days of the year, I was in full summer gear, barefoot, denim shorts on and a very loose vest/tank top. She came into my reading room and I conducted the reading for her.

At the end of the session she thanked me for a beautiful reading, but also said how sorry she felt for me. I was a little bit taken aback by that comment. She went onto say how she felt so sorry for me that I had needed to cause such mutilation to my body. I realised at that point she was talking about my tattoos. Being that it was so hot my arms were on full show. I simply smiled and said, "well, tattoos are not for everyone and whilst you may view them as scars upon the body, for me they are so much more than that".

Each piece of inked artwork holds a power and story of its own. Each piece is a reflection of part of my development journey of life that I have gone and will continue to go through. My purple feather upon my wrist holds significant magick for me. When I had that done I did my first ever full day of readings within a tattoo studio. This was a place called White Horse Tattoo Studio in Hungerford.

For me that day held real power and unconditional love. A few things took place that day, the first being I met a lovely soul, Evelyn who ran the place. Perhaps one of the most gifted and true spiritual friends I am blessed to know. The second thing that happened spirit really showed me that they truly wanted me to work for them. Just the fact that the studio was called the White Horse I found powerful, as at the time I was living in Westbury in Wiltshire and my house was literally just below the chalked white horse. The final piece of magick was that Evelyn did a trade for me which I am eternal blessed and grateful for. A reading in exchange for a tattoo. My tattooed feather is my dedication to my spirit team, and my spirit work.

As time went on me and Evelyn formed a beautiful working relationship and friendship and I was often a guest reader at her tattoo studio, she also had an amazing healing room called Heart Song - that's where I later did the bulk of my readings and workshops. As time went on the overheads where increasing and Evelyn decided to close the doors and find a new space to pursue her own spirit magick. I did a final day of readings at the venue, and it was just as magical as the day we first met. We ended up doing another trade and I had my witches' protection artwork done on my other wrist. Equally powerful and important for me. A dedication of my witchcraft and also a tattoo of spiritual and magical protection for self.

So, to go back to my lovely client you may see my ink as just scars upon the skin, but they are authentic pieces of artwork that hold so much love and power from within. Just because you may not like something or even fully understand it, that is OK and your choice and own freewill. But it does not affect any form of my reading work, or my ability to deliver a message. I will not apologise or feel ashamed of my ink art, as for me they represent my life and my own eternal spirit.

If You're Waiting For Someone To Believe In you, You'll Be Waiting Forever. You Must Believe In Yourself – Cher

Unconditional Love

People often ask me as a spiritual medium, does God exist?

I can only answer this from my own awareness and level of working with the spirit world for the time that I have been blessed to do so.

The answer to this question is quite simple… Yes, God does exist. But God is a personal subject matter for each of us. For me God is not some biblical guy floating on the clouds wearing a white robe, holding an ancient bible. God is so much more than just what a preset religion would have you believe.

For me… God is all around us. God is the beautiful planet that we are blessed to live upon, the trees that give us the breath of life, that ask for little to nothing in return. God is the beautiful earth beneath our feet and Mother Earth's temples of nature to protect, worship, admire and enjoy. God is the beautiful animals that we come to know and love.

God is the pure sunlight shining in through a window of morning lighting up a new day. Or the moon cleansing and protecting the night sky, whilst we lay our eyes to rest and fall asleep. God is the changing of the seasons, and the elements that we embrace throughout the year.

God is the rising waves of a beautiful ocean or sea. Or the green grass in a beautiful meadow or garden.

God is the power of truth the words we seek and speak. God is unconditional love within your heart centre and mine.

God is everywhere, the universe; we are all creations of God and an ongoing work in progress.

God is the power of your own intentions, and the way you choose to live your life whilst here within this time and space. God is your own moral compass and you hold the freedom of where you choose to point and use it.

God is the spirit world, that higher vibration or frequency to that of our own. God is the realm of eternal love, light and inner peace.

God is the laughter within your belly, or the smile that lights up another smile around you. Or the music that lights up your day and makes you want to dance freely around a room.

God is the power to love hard, forgive fast and often and enjoy all the wonders the world has to offer.

God is true Spirit Magick

You are God, and God is you

I hope you have enjoyed the teachings and learnings within this book. I do not hold all the answers and I do not consider myself to be of greater importance to another. All I know is that I am someone that is blessed to call themselves a spiritual medium, a psychic, a tarot reader, a healer and a male witch. Spirit have entrusted me with these gifts for me to use and work with, within this lifetime. I am a follower of the old ways. A time when love was free, and the world was young and beautiful.

One final thing I wish to share with you is one of the hardest jobs you will find as a psychic or medium is trying to correct broken energy. The amount of times I have had to deliver messages from the spirit world saying sorry to family members or friends whom have done wrong, or who are trying to apologise for behaviours that can never be mended.

Perhaps of all the lessons we are all here on earth to learn is the lesson and power of forgiveness.

If you yourself are in a family feud or are holding onto anger over a person or circumstance allow the energy of forgiveness in. Not to forgive or forget what you have been put through. But to allow eternal inner peace into your own heart centre to set yourself and those that bind you free.

We are all walking this earth on extremely borrowed time, use the time you are gifted within your own hourglass well, for once it's gone, you will never get it back.

Blessed be dear reader.

Until we meet again.

Love Always

Mitch x

Hate No One, No Matter How Much They've Wronged You. Live Humbly, No Matter How Wealthy You Become. Think Positively, No Matter How Hard Life Is. Give Much, Even If You've Been Given Little. Forgive All, Especially Yourself. And Never Stop Praying For The Best For Everyone – Ali Ibn Abi Talib

Blessings

I would like to say a huge thank you to those beautiful souls that have continued to support my work in all its formats and areas. As ever a heartfelt thank you to my spirit guides, angels, door keepers and helpers.

I would like to say thank you to Sharon Chalk – Editor

Vicky Baker – Front Cover Artwork

Today Walk The Path Pure And True
May The World's Love Come To You
Look Ahead Not Behind
See Tomorrow's Possibility In Your Mind
See Your Purpose Strong And Bold
Give Three Blessings For Each One You Hold
Dream Of Love And Peace Tonight
Wake Tomorrow In Blessed Light

Printed in Poland
by Amazon Fulfillment
Poland Sp. z o.o., Wrocław